Creation *versus* Evolution? NOT REALLY!

William A. Schmeling

CLAYTON PUBLISHING HOUSE
P. O. Box 9258
St. Louis, Missouri 63117

Clayton Publishing House, St. Louis, Missouri

For Sherman

and the others

who asked

CONTENTS

ACKNOWLEDGMENT

The writer acknowledges and thanks the Division of Education and Ministry of the National Council of the Churches of Christ in the U.S.A. for their kind permission to quote from the Revised Standard Version Bible in this work.

This little book addresses a big question, <u>What</u> <u>do</u> <u>you</u> <u>do</u> with <u>creation</u> and <u>evolution</u>? The question is important because it deeply bothers so many people. In my years as a religion instructor at a Lutheran high school, the question was asked repeatedly by young Christians struggling to sharpen their understanding of God and the world into a faith that really "worked" for them. As a parish pastor, I've had the same question raised by college students looking for some reconciliation between their old assumptions in the church and their new discoveries in the science classroom. The apparent conflict between creation and evolution has become a major hurdle for many in getting on to those God/people and people/people relationships that Christianity is all about. <u>How</u> <u>do</u> <u>you</u> <u>reconcile</u> <u>science</u> <u>and</u> <u>the</u> <u>Bible</u>?

This book is an expanded version of the answer I have given on those occasions. You will observe that there are few footnotes here. The reason for that is two-fold. First, I honestly can't remember the persons and books to which I am indebted for each little facet of the themes I have pulled together here. Second, this is not intended to be a monumental resource book for professional Old Testament scholars. The purpose of the book is much more modest. It is to present as simply as possible some answers and directions that have proved helpful to young friends who were troubled by the apparent conflict between Bible and science. I hope they are answers and directions that will prove helpful to you as well.

I believe the real problem behind the question we're addressing is not with the Bible itself nor with science itself, but with faulty definitions and assumptions we have about the Bible and science. The point of this book is that both Bible and science are true. They are not classic enemies locked in mortal combat. Neither has to out-do the other in order to win, to be safe, or to prove something to the world. Creation and evolution are complementary truths (that is, one fulfills the other), not antagonistic.

I recognize that there are parts of Christendom today where such statements immediately dump one from the sheep fold into the goat pen and brand one a "Bible doubter", case unheard. That is most unfortunate. It is precisely Bible believing that moves me to answer the question as I shall attempt to do.

The words of St. Augustine are instructive here. Long ago he said, "Let us doubt without disbelief the things to be believed." Good saying. He recognized 1) that it is simply the human "way" to question, to wonder, to doubt, to probe to the limits of one's imagination and understanding, and 2) that it is simply God's way to bring our doubts and probings home to Him apart from Whom our hearts are restless. God gave us minds to use in the very process of our Bible believing. To search and probe the creation accounts, to ask questions of their meaning and purpose, is not to undermine God, Church or Bible. It is rather to come to renewed faith in God who creates and sustains heaven and earth.

Whatever else proves helpful and useful to you in this book, may that strengthened and renewed faith be yours!

All Saints' Day

CHAPTER 1

DEFINITIONS

The question, "How do you reconcile creation and evolution?" means that for the inquirer, Bible and science
seem to be antagonistic, contradictory and potentially
irreconcilable. Maybe it's in the way we were raised. Somewhere along the line we were all given definitions of
"Bible" and "science" that seem to suggest more problems
than they solve. Many of us wind up with a blind, unques-
tioning loyalty to a school of interpretation. This is not
necessarily the same as loyalty to God or even loyalty to
that Book which we accept as His Word. It is loyalty to
one possible way of approaching and understanding that Book.
Before we look at the creation accounts, then, we should
first distinguish between the "loads" we expect the Bible
and science to carry.

THE BIBLE

The Bible is the Word of God. It is "inspired by God
and profitable for teaching, for reproof, for correction,
and for training in righteousness, that the man of God may
be complete, equipped for every good work." (2 Timothy 3:
16, 17) By Paul's definition here, the Bible is a guide

Creation <u>Versus</u> Evolution? Not Really!

for life with God and a compendium of truth to outfit us for life under God. For this job description it is trustworthy, authoritative, and without error.

It is impossible to talk about the Bible these days without getting into that briar patch of inspiration. What the apostles and prophets were perfectly willing to leave as one word, we who follow in their train have seen fit to belabor into whole paragraphs. Denominations, congregations, families and individual careers throughout Christendom are strewn with the gore and carnage of sincere, but allegedly unavoidable, battles over just how and to what extent the Bible was and is inspired. I suspect the angels themselves prefer not to tread here, but come, let us rush in.

When I was very young, I'm sure I believed the King James Bible fell out of heaven one day. I call this belief the "grass roots" school of inspiration. Complete with Ussher's chronology, rainbow cover, concordance and Bible helps, and with Jesus' exact words printed in red, the "Saint James Version" fell into the Court of St. James, "Beautifully illustrated and self-pronouncing."

That of course is untrue, as fellow Christians helped me to understand. We know the Bible came to us as the Word of God through the earthen vessels of people like ourselves. It came in fits and leaps, in different ages, as separate scrolls, and in three languages - Hebrew, Aramaic and a good measure of Street Greek. We know it was handed down for generations in copies and in copies of copies. Copies of those copies were copied by forgotten hosts of scribes and monks for use in the community of the faithful, because the Word was (and is) important. Somewhere along the line, men of God, confident that the Spirit was with them, "voted" on which books should be pulled together to form the Bible - the canon. The Jewish teachers met at Jamnia in A.D. 90 and prayerfully decided that the thirty-nine books we call the Old Testament were the Word of God. By usage, most Christians have always agreed that the canon of the scholars of Jamnia lists the correct Scriptures. Genesis as we have it is a part of the Word of God. What we call the New Testament was pulled together by the decision of Christian bishops meeting at Carthage around A.D. 400, but that's beside the point. For the purposes of this book, we need note only that Genesis, as we have it, has been accepted in all times, in all places, and by all believers, as a part of the inspired Word of God.

There is a "mechanical" school of inspiration that seems unduly dedicated to pinning down exactly how the Word was inspired. Many a confirmation class gets the idea that the Holy Spirit used something like a telephone, thus: (Ring. Ring.) "Hello, Isaiah? The Lord here. Say, Isaiah, you got a minute? Just thought of some great judgments and promises. I've been reworking the stuff I sent Micah last week. Got your pen ready? Good. Now get this down exactly. Word for Word, or else! 'The vision of Isaiah the son of Amoz, which he...'"

You say that's absurd? I tell you there are Christian young people who are led by the mechanical school to believe that it happened just that way and no other. It is far better to leave inspiration where the angels do. The Word _is_ inspired. Let us not presume to bedevil the how of it.

Let me commend to your reading the article on inspiration in the old Lutheran Cyclopedia. Though the article covers several pages in its detailed coverage of the topic, it is the first sentence that contains the best definition of inspiration I've run across:

> By confessing the doctrine of inspiration, we declare our belief...that the Holy Spirit exercised a special influence by which He guided His chosen instruments to speak the things He desired them to speak, and to write the things He desired them to write...[1]

Isn't that beautiful? That way Paul could write like Paul, Matthew could write like Matthew, David could write like David, and so on. Styles of writing, personal fixations

Creation <u>Versus</u> Evolution? Not Really!

on "what is important," views of the world, motives for
"packaging" the truth each in his individual way, could
differ according to the writers' personalities and according to the situations and ages they were addressing. In
it all, however, in all its holy earthen-vesselness, what
they wrote was still consistent with what the Holy Spirit
desired them to write. What could be less labored or more
profound?

The point is that Christianity possesses a revealed
theology. We have the Bible, including Genesis, as a history of salvation, to equip us toward Christian completeness. It is a <u>theological</u> book. That means it is answering
questions about God and man. Who is God? Who am I? What
is the relationship between us? Why am I here? Why is anything here? What is life all about? Where am I going?
Does it make any difference? In answer to these questions
and many more, holy truth is wholly true.

SCIENCE

Now let me give you my "layman's" definition of science.
Though I've heard it prefixed as "godless" science more than
once in Christian circles, I don't believe science is the
great adversary of holy truth. Nor does the scientist.
Science is simply the pursuit of empirical knowledge. The
scientist looks at facts, data, and phenomena, measuring
them with the most precise instruments of the age, aiming
at accurate description of the findings. The scientist
labels, records, hypothesizes and theorizes about cause and
effect relationships. As they deal with the question of how
people got here, scientists examine the empirical evidence
at hand and then suggest "working explanations" for things
as they see them. These working explanations, however, re-
main just that - theories - unless they can be verified by
measurement or demonstration. The purview of science is
that truth which can be measured by the instruments now
available. Science asks the questions of "what" and "how".
What is it? What does it look like? What does it do? How
does it react? How did it get here? How do I know? For
such questions science is wholly true in so far as its as-
sessments of the matter can be verified.

14

You see, then, we're dealing with different kinds of
truth. The Bible speaks its truth in the revealed answers
to the great "who" and "why" questions of life. Science
has its truth in the demonstrable answers and theories con-
cerning the "what" and "how" of things. The two kinds of
truth exist side by side. Neither is aiming to put the
other out of commission. I want to develop this thought
more fully later, but for the present it will be helpful to
move on to a study of creation as presented in the book of
Genesis. In the light of that study, the peaceful co-exis-
tence of Biblical truth and scientific truth can appear
much more clearly.

CHAPTER 2

THE BIBLICAL CREATION ACCOUNTS

Right! Accounts. Plural. There are two creation accounts back-to-back in Genesis. Another, a chorale on the
wonders of nature, appears in Psalm 104. Still another, an
aria on man as the viceroy of God, is in Proverbs 8. Scattered throughout the Bible are further bits and pieces of
theological beauty on the purpose, nature and operation of
created phenomena and of humankind.

It is the first two accounts in particular that give
many people the most trouble. It's easy to see that Psalms,
Proverbs and Ecclesiastes are poetic - not intended to be
taken as "scientifically" literal. With Genesis, however,
many assume that here the Bible is presenting the story of
creation in factual prose, so "scientifically" accurate that
news cameras would have picked it up just this way if cameras had been invented at that time. Let's examine the
Genesis accounts and see if this is the case.

Take out your Bible; the particular version doesn't
really matter. Read all of Genesis 1 and 2. Take your time;
read carefully.

Creation <u>Versus</u> Evolution? Not Really!

Do you see how the two accounts disagree in important detail? The physical data, the description of how long, in what way, and in what order things "got here" in the one account is very different from these particulars in the other account. On the other hand, the two accounts agree, fulfill, and complement one another in forming a profound theological statement. It must be that the <u>theological</u> statement is what the authors are driving at.

What two accounts, you say? Where does one stop and the other begin? What two authors? Very clever, our ancients. Verse 4 of chapter 2 splits both ways. It's the end of the first account and the beginning of the second account. This division shows up clearly in the Revised Standard Version and even more markedly in the Jerusalem Bible, but the King James Bible weaves the words all together so beautifully that you don't notice the "seam" there without a lot of probing.

I have borrowed and adapted a little graph from a truly beautiful handling of these chapters that appeared in a church publication for high school youth.[2]

	First Account Genesis 1-2:4a	Second Account Genesis 2:4b-25
Title of Creator	"God" ("Elohim")	"LORD God" ("Yahweh Elohim")
Method of Creating	Fiat - Command "God said, let there be..." "God created man..."	Action - Involvement "God made... formed... took... caused..."
Time Element	Six 24-hour days. God rested on the seventh day.	Indeterminate. "In the day..."
Order of Man's Creation	Man (and woman) created last, after all plants and animals.	Man created first, before plants and animals. Woman created last.

Creation Versus Evolution? Not Really!

Such a graph helps us to see things we might ordinarily miss. Now read Genesis 1 and 2 again, checking for the particulars to which this graph calls our attention. Read the creation accounts in several versions.

Notice that in the first chapter and the next three verses God is always called "God". (The Hebrew for "God" is "Elohim".) Beginning at Genesis 2:4b, the Creator is consistently called "LORD God" ("YAHWEH Elohim".) You have two different names or titles, each used with unfailing consistency on its particular side of the "seam" in Genesis 2:4.

There are also two different methods of creation. In the first account, creation consistently comes into being by the command or fiat of God, until He creates man in His image in 1:27. In the second account, the LORD, YAHWEH, commands little or nothing in the creative process. He does it "by hand", not by creative word. He is the picture of the celestial Artisan, "up to here" in clay. The verbs of creating in the second account are action verbs - involvement down in the thing itself: "made...formed...breathed... made to grow...planted...took...formed...caused to fall... took...made."

The time element in the first account is six precise days - evening and morning - twenty-four hours each, presumably. On the seventh day, God rests from His word of commanding, which, incidentally, sets the precedent for Israel's resting on the seventh day in a later chapter of salvation history. The time element in the second account is indeterminate and, presumably, unimportant for the purposes of that writer. One day is the only temporal element suggested: "In the day that the LORD God made the earth and the heavens..."

Man appears at a different place in the accounts. In the first account, all creation is called forth into being to set the stage for God's opus maius, the creation of humankind, in verse 27. Male and female are created simultaneously. Both are equally blessed, and both are given

equal jurisdiction over creation. ("That" tree and prohibitions about its fruit are to be found nowhere in this
account.) Strikingly different is the order of things in
the second story. When nothing was growing anywhere because there wasn't any rain, God formed man out of the
dust. He breathed into him the breath of life. Then Yahweh planted a garden in Eden, complete with the forbidden
tree, and He put man into the garden. Because man needed
company, God then created all the rest of the animals and
brought them to the man for naming. Among all these beasts,
however, there was no suitable mate for man. Solution?
A second act of special creation! With heavy sleep as the
anesthetic, God operated on man, extracted a rib, healed
the wound, and fashioned woman out of the rib.[3]

What are these writers driving at? If we say their in-
tention is to describe the origin and appearance of natural
phenomena, to give physically accurate detail, we're in
trouble. In the last quarter of the twentieth century, we
simply don't work with the cosmology of the first chapter,
nor with the geography of the second. Rather, these accounts are theological statements about God and people, and
about the relationship between the two. God is Creator,
any way you read either account. Humankind is His special
creation, any way you read either account. God and humankind have a unique interrelationship and interresponsibili-
ty, any way you read either account.

Thus: Is God transcendent - apart, disengaged from
natural phenomena, "spiritual" - as suggested in the first
account? Or is He immanent - involved, close, "personal" -
as in the second? The answer is obvious: He's both! He
is the untouchable, unknowable, unapproachable, Wholly and
Holy Other, and He is the Lover, Preserver, Helper, Healer,
closer than the air we breathe. How deficient one picture
or idea of God would be without the other! How imbalanced
man's knowledge of God, as well as his relationship to God,
would be without both aspects of His self-revelation!

Similarly, is humankind the apex of God's creation, to
which all else was leading, as in the first account?

21

Creation <u>Versus</u> Evolution? Not Really!

Or did man come first, and everything else later, as in the second account? The timing of humankind's appearance does not seem to be the major point either of the accounts is making. Whether people are first or last is not the thing that makes them theologically "special". They are special because God made them special. They are uniquely related to their Creator and uniquely placed over the rest of creation. Humanity gets more "place" and privilege from God, more relationship to God, and also more responsibility under God.

Both statements, the affirmation of God as Creator and the uniqueness of humankind as special creation, are theological statements. They are beyond the realm and purview of science because they are matters that simply cannot be tested by scientific method and instrument at this time. They are matters of faith; one either believes them or rejects them. The Biblical accounts are answering questions that science is not asking: Who is God? Who is man? How are we related? Why am I here? What is life all about? Why do I have problems? Where am I going? So what?

The two accounts are quite different in structure and detail. The first is liturgical; beautifully balanced, repetitive as a litany. It seems suitable for chanting in the Temple or at some festival of creation. The second account is narrative, gutsy, down-home, and - in the strict sense of the word - "fabulous" (like a fable or an epic folk tale). It seems uniquely suited to round-the-campfire or at-the-dinner-table discussions of why people feel as they do toward God and how this relationship came about. Taken separately and taken together, both accounts make profound theological statements of truths perceivable to and receivable by faith alone.

In this light, the physical data in the accounts are meant to be no more than incidental "setting" to make the theological point. If the physical descriptions in the creation accounts were meant to be the writers' major points, then we have two problems. First, the information is different in each account, and, second, the information

is simply untenable in the light of present knowledge about
the universe. There is no disrespect for God or the Bible
in saying this. Both accounts are scientifically primitive.
They are pre-logical. Profound and eternal as theology,
they are dated as descriptions of cosmology and geography.

Certainly that's a "heavy" statement, but it can be
tested by diagramming the accounts as they are given That's
why it is important to read the accounts as they are given,
without trying to read our post-Copernican cosmology into
them. That would do violence to the pre-Ptolemaic text.

A word about the art work to follow: the sketches here
are far more primitive than the first writer probably envisioned things as he was writing. Parts of the drawings
are out of scale. I am only trying to diagram the physical
information presented, as a visual help; so use your imagination to get a feel for the total picture.

Creation <u>Versus</u> Evolution? Not Really!

THE FIRST CREATION ACCOUNT

IN THE BEGINNING

Genesis 1:1,2

In the beginning God created the heavens and the earth. The earth was without form and void, and darkness was upon the face of the deep; and the Spirit of God was moving over the face of the waters.

Creation <u>Versus</u> Evolution? Not Really!

THE FIRST DAY

Genesis 1:3-5

*And God said, "Let there be light"; and there was light.
And God saw that the light was good; and God separated
the light from the darkness. God called the light Day,
and the darkness he called Night. And there was evening
and there was morning, one day.*

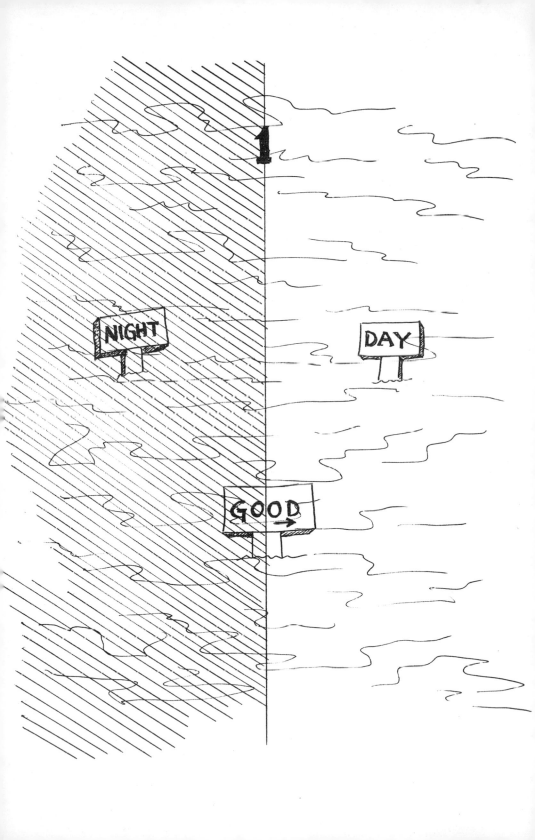

THE SECOND DAY

Genesis 1:6-8

And God said, "Let there be a firmament in the midst of the waters, and let it separate the waters from the waters." And God made the firmament and separated the waters which were under the firmament from the waters which were above the firmament. And it was so. And God called the firmament Heaven. And there was evening and there was morning, a second day.

WATERS ABOVE FIRMAMENT

THE FIRMAMENT →

2

EVENING   MORNING

WATERS   UNDER

FIRMAMENT

THE THIRD DAY

Genesis 1:9-13

And God said, "Let the waters under the heavens be gathered together into one place, and let the dry land appear." And it was so. God called the dry land Earth, and the waters that were gathered together he called Seas. And God saw that it was good. And God said, "Let the earth put forth vegetation, plants yielding seed, and fruit trees bearing fruit in which is their seed, each according to its kind, upon the earth." And it was so. The earth brought forth vegetation, plants yielding seed according to their own kinds, and trees bearing fruit in which is their seed, each according to its kind. And God saw that it was good. And there was evening and there was morning, a third day.

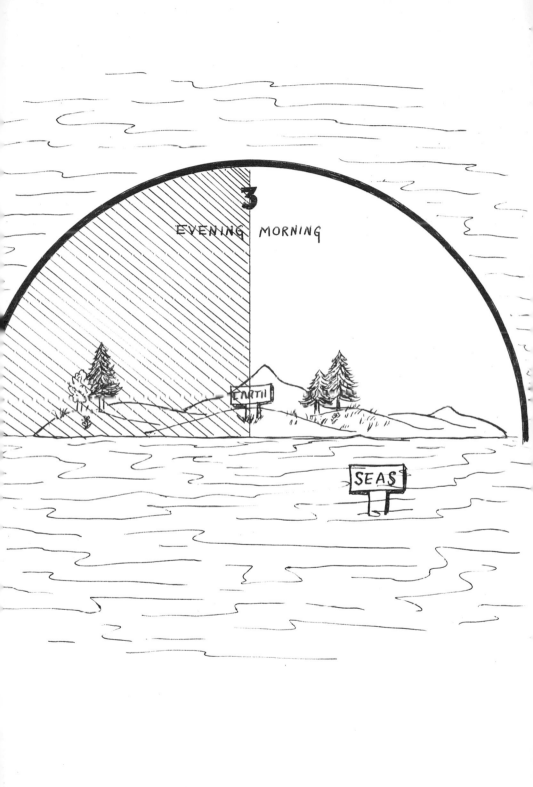

THE FOURTH DAY

Genesis 1:14-19

And God said, "Let there be lights in the firmament of the heavens to separate the day from the night; and let them be for signs and for seasons and for days and years, and let them be lights in the firmament of the heavens to give light upon the earth." And it was so. And God made the two great lights, the greater light to rule the day, and the lesser light to rule the night; he made the stars also. And God set them in the firmament of the heavens to give light upon the earth, to rule over the day and over the night, and to separate the light from the darkness. And God saw that it was good. And there was evening and there was morning, a fourth day.

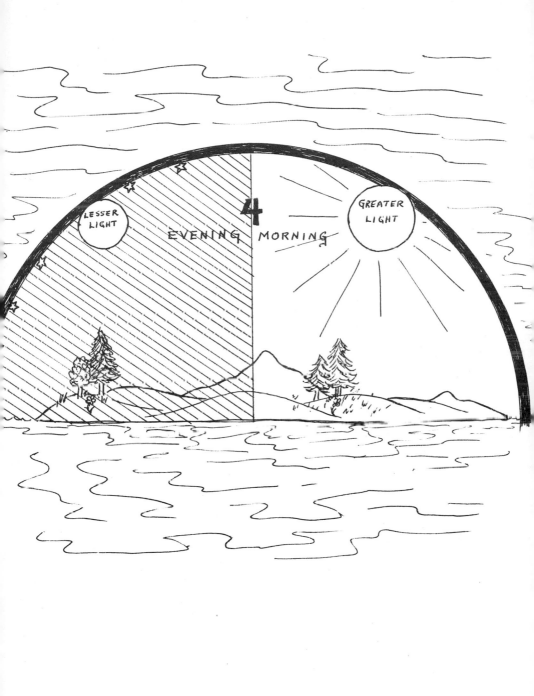

THE FIFTH DAY

Genesis 1:20-23

And God said, "Let the waters bring forth swarms of living creatures, and let birds fly above the earth across the firmament of the heavens." So God created the great sea monsters and every living creature that moves, with which the waters swarm, according to their kinds, and every winged bird according to its kind. And God saw that it was good. And God blessed them saying, "Be fruitful and multiply and fill the waters in the seas, and let birds multiply on the earth." And there was evening and there was morning, a fifth day.

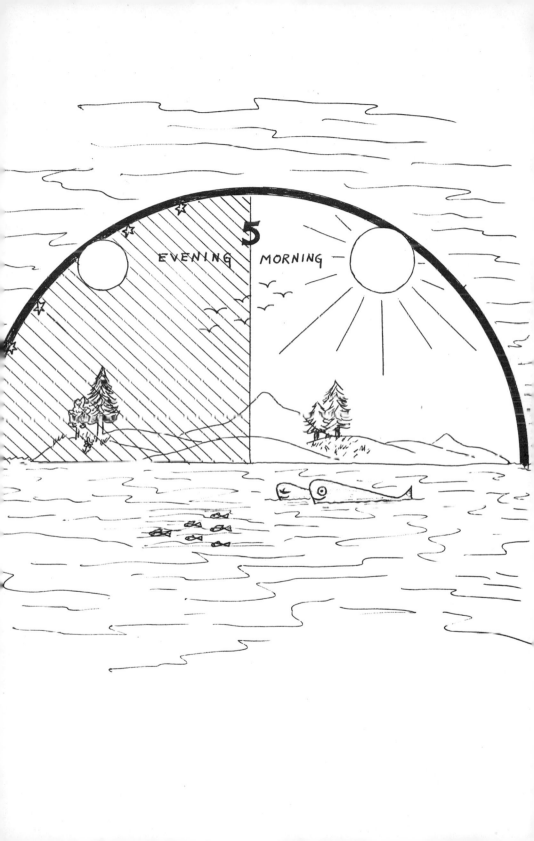

THE SIXTH DAY, PART ONE

Genesis 1:24, 25

And God said, "Let the earth bring forth living creatures according to their kinds: cattle and creeping things and beasts of the earth according to their kinds." And it was so. And God made the beasts of the earth according to their kinds and the cattle according to their kinds, and everything that creeps upon the ground according to its kind. And God saw that it was good.

THE SIXTH DAY, PART TWO

Genesis 1:26-31

Then God said, "Let us make man in our image, after our likeness; and let them have dominion over the fish of the sea, and over the birds of the air, and over the cattle, and over all the earth, and over every creeping thing that creeps upon the earth." So God created man in his own image, in the image of God he created him; male and female he created them. And God blessed them, and God said to them, "Be fruitful and multiply, and fill the earth and subdue it; and have dominion over the fish of the sea and over the birds of the air and over every living thing that moves upon the earth." And God said, "Behold, I have given you every plant yielding seed which is upon the face of all the earth, and every tree with seed in its fruit; you shall have them for food. And to every beast of the earth, and to every bird of the air, and to everything that creeps on the earth, everything that has the breath of life, I have given every green plant for food." And it was so. And God saw everything that he had made, and behold, it was very good. And there was evening and there was morning, a sixth day.

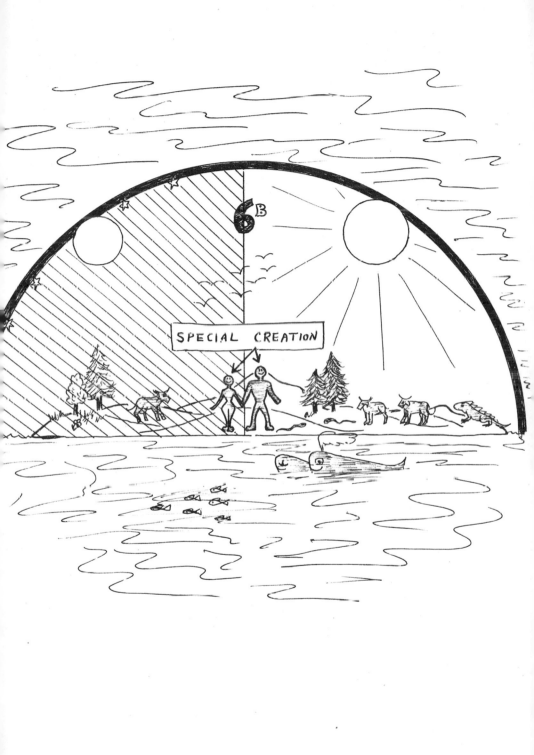

THE SEVENTH DAY

Genesis 2:1-4a

Thus the heavens and the earth were finished, and all the host of them. And on the seventh day God finished his work which he had done, and he rested on the seventh day from all his work which he had done. So God blessed the seventh day and hallowed it, because on it God rested from all his work which he had done in creation.

These are the generations of the heavens and the earth when they were created.

Creation Versus Evolution? Not Really!

To diagram the second account calls for a different approach. Here it is impossible to stand back and see everything on one scale. Like a modern camera crew, we have to zero in on the action with our zoom lens, then back off for the larger picture, then zoom in again. There is no sky dome and ordered picture of the universe, with God calling life into being from afar. Rather, we have God within His creation - immanent, operating, doing, planting.

THE SECOND ACCOUNT

Genesis 2:4b-6

In the day that the LORD God made the earth and the heavens, when no plant of the field was yet in the earth and no herb of the field had yet sprung up - for the LORD God had not caused it to rain upon the earth, and there was no man to till the ground; but a mist went up from the earth and watered the whole face of the ground...

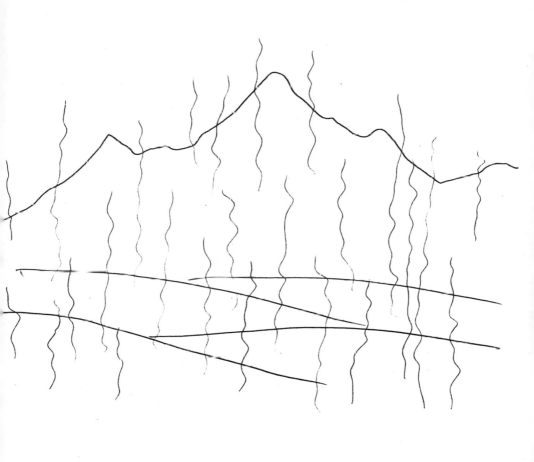

Creation <u>Versus</u> Evolution? Not Really!

Genesis 2:7

then the LORD God formed man of dust from the ground, and breathed into his nostrils the breath of life; and man became a living being.

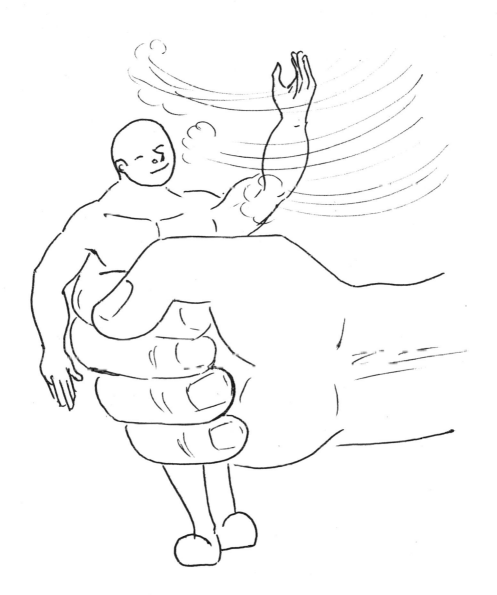

Creation <u>Versus</u> Evolution? Not Really!

Genesis 2:8a

And the LORD God planted a garden in Eden, in the east;

Creation <u>Versus</u> Evolution? Not Really!

Genesis 2:8b

and there he put the man whom he had formed.

Creation <u>Versus</u> Evolution? Not Really!

Genesis 2:9

And out of the ground the LORD God made to grow every tree that is pleasant to the sight and good for food, the tree of life also in the midst of the garden, and the tree of the knowledge of good and evil.

Genesis 2:10-14

*A river flowed out of Eden to water the garden, and there
it divided and became four rivers. The name of the first
is Pishon; it is the one which flows around the whole land
of Havilah, where there is gold; and the gold of that land
is good; bdellium and onyx stone are there. The name of
the second river is Gihon; it is the one which flows
around the whole land of Cush. And the name of the third
river is Hiddekel, which flows east of Assyria. And the
fourth river is the Euphrates.*

(With this information, it is impossible to draw a map so
that it corresponds with present geographical knowledge.
See the outline map of the middle east and its rivers in
the inset at the lower right corner of the page.)

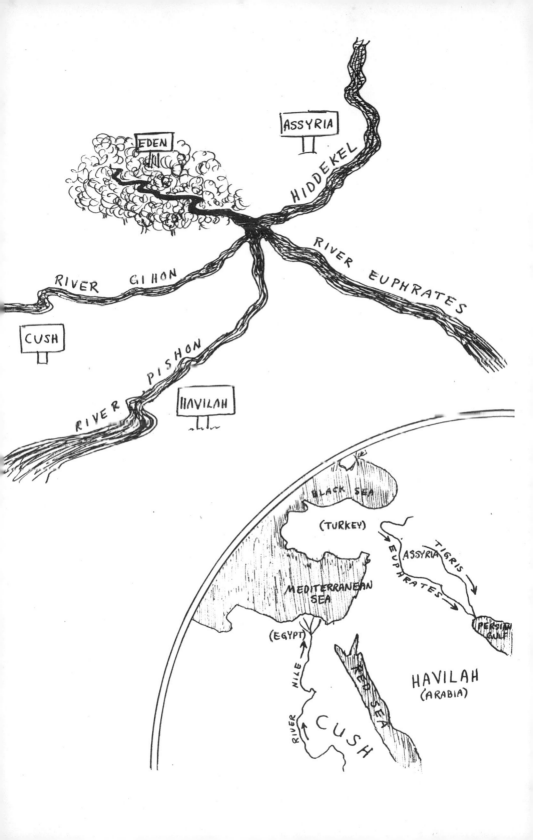

Creation <u>Versus</u> Evolution? Not Really!

Genesis 2:15-17

The LORD God took the man and put him in the garden of Eden to till it and keep it. And the LORD God commanded the man saying, "You may freely eat of every tree of the garden; but of the tree of the knowledge of good and evil you shall not eat, for in the day that you eat of it you shall die."

Creation <u>Versus</u> Evolution? Not Really!

Genesis 2:18-20

Then the LORD God said, "It is not good that the man should be alone; I will make him a helper fit for him." So out of the ground the LORD God formed every beast of the field and every bird of the air, and brought them to the man to see what he would call them; and whatever the man called every living creature, that was its name. The man gave names to all cattle, and to the birds of the air, and to every beast of the field; but for the man there was not found a helper fit for him.

Genesis 2:21-25

*So the LORD God caused a deep sleep to fall upon the man,
and while he slept took one of his ribs and closed up its
place with flesh; and the rib which the LORD God had taken
from the man he made into a woman and brought her to the
man. Then the man said, "This at last is bone of my bones
and flesh of my flesh; She shall be called Woman, because
she was taken out of Man."*

*Therefore a man leaves his father and his mother and cleaves
to his wife, and they become one flesh. And the man and his
wife were both naked, and were not ashamed.*

Creation <u>Versus</u> Evolution? Not Really!

MORE COSMOLOGICAL DETAIL

The second account continues on into chapter three of Genesis, with the story of the temptation and fall of mankind. For the purposes of this book, though, let's leave the second account here and back up to the diagram of the universe on the seventh day of the first account (page 41). From other parts of the Old Testament we can flesh out that basic diagram of the world as our pre-Ptolemaic fathers envisioned it. The first nine verses of Psalm 104 give us, in poetic language, a picture of the world that God has created and still preserves. A diagram of this "paean of creation" fits right in with the diagram of the first Genesis account.

Psalm 104:1-9

Bless the LORD, O my soul! O LORD my God, thou art very great! Thou art clothed with honor and majesty, who coverest thyself with light as with a garment, who hast stretched out the heavens like a tent, who hast laid the beams of thy chambers on the waters, who makest the clouds thy chariot, who ridest on the wings of the wind, who makest the winds thy messengers, fire and flame thy ministers.

Thou didst set the earth on its foundations, so that it should never be shaken. Thou didst cover it with the deep as with a garment; the waters stood above the mountains. At thy rebuke they fled; at the sound of thy thunder they took to flight. The mountains rose, the valleys sank down to the place which thou didst appoint for them. Thou didst set a bound which they should not pass, so that they might not again cover the earth.

GOD'S CHAMBERS

BEAMS

THE WATERS

THE WATERS

THE HEAVENS STRETCHED OUT AS A TENT

PATH OF THE SUN

GOD'S CHARIOT

WIND MESSENGER

FIRE & FLAME MESSENGERS

PLACE WHERE SUN RISES

BOUNDARY SET FOR THE SEA

FOUNDATIONS

THE DEEP

SHEOL (THE PIT)

PASSAGEWAY FOR THE SUN?

Creation <u>Versus</u> Evolution? Not Really!

From Ecclesiastes 1:5-7, we could add to the diagram some sort of underground or underwater passageway for the sun to travel through during the night so that it might rise again in the east, and we can add some sort of underground irrigation system for streams to return from the ocean to their points of origin. From many of the Psalms (for example, Psalm 30:3, 9; Psalm 18:4) we could add the realm of the dead, Sheol, where both good and bad go when life on the surface of the earth is finished. The pre-Ptolemaic cosmology is now complete.

Is this an accurate (empirically precise) cosmology? No. Not on the basis of our present knowledge of the universe. Is it true? That is, is it a paean of praise to the God who made all things and who reveals to the eyes of the faithful something of Himself and His Majesty in the marvels of the cosmos? Yes, of course it is true. Taken literally, as definitive science, it would run counter to everything we know about the universe today. Taken figuratively, as descriptive verse on the wonder of God reflected in the wonder of His handiwork, it is true. Very true. And timelessly profound.

Most people have no difficulty in seeing Psalms and Ecclesiastes as poetic. ("Well of course God doesn't ride around on the clouds; that's just a poetic way of saying...") It is when we miss the fact that Genesis 1 is also poetry that we make difficulties for ourselves. If we read Genesis 1 literally, as a "scientific" account, then the correct idea of the shape of the cosmos should look pretty much as we have diagrammed it for the sixth day (page 39). Is this honestly the shape of the world as we know it? Is the universe earth-centered, with a sky vault (firmament) holding in check all those threatening waters just beyond it, with the sun, moon, and planets coursing around in their appointed channels in or within that sky vault? The answer, of course, is no. Our everyday working idea of the earth and its place in the heavens is something more like this:

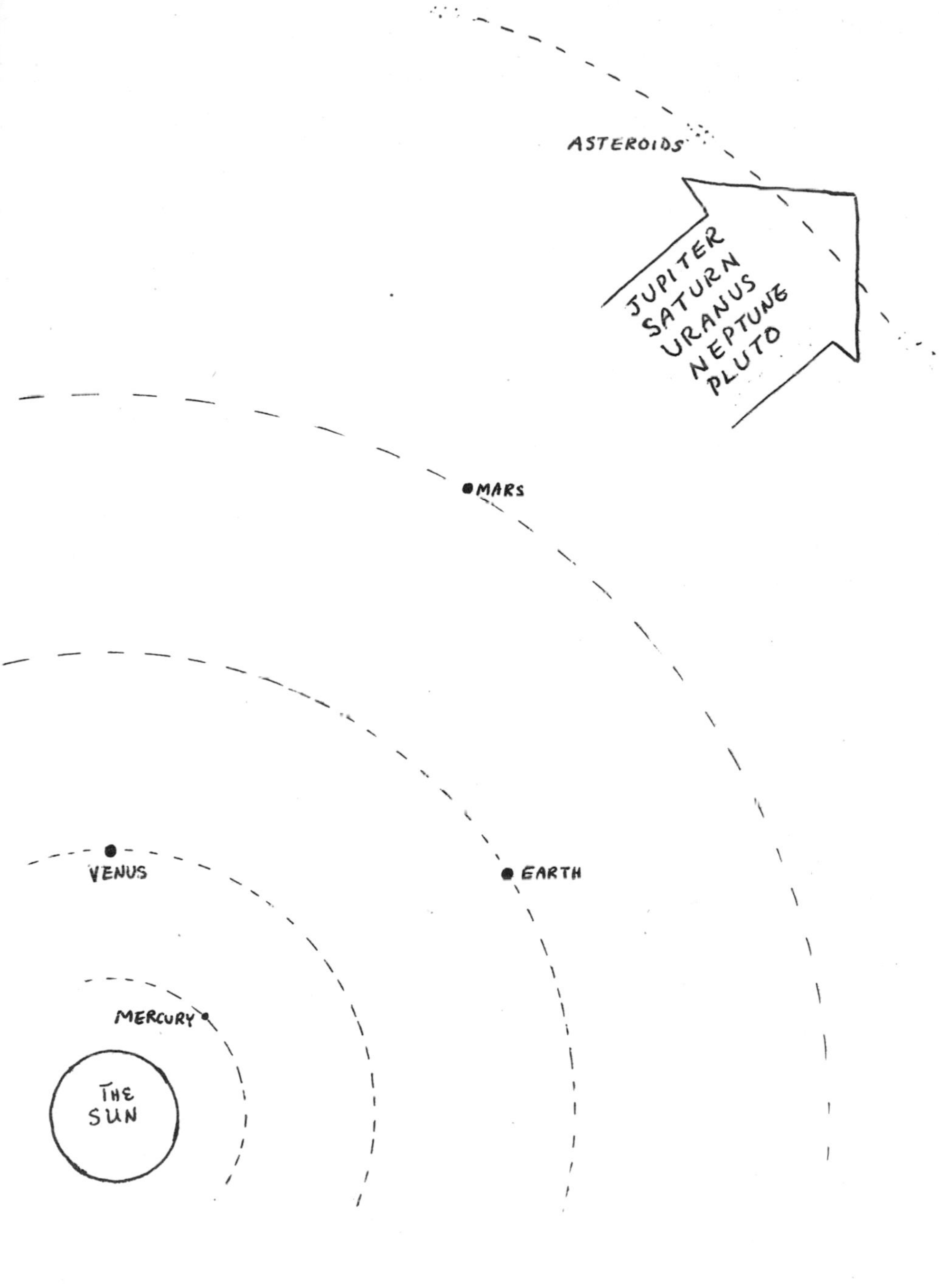

ASTEROIDS
JUPITER
SATURN
URANUS
NEPTUNE
PLUTO
MARS
VENUS
EARTH
MERCURY
THE SUN

Creation Versus Evolution? Not Really!

On the basis of empirically verifiable data, we think of our earth as an ovoid making its annual orbit around the sun. We know that we are but one of several planets making their several revolutions around this particular star. We know that our moon is our own satellite, revolving around us.

In the bigger picture we know that our entire solar system is but a speck at the periphery of one spiral galaxy. If you took a map of the whole galaxy and reduced the scale to the size of this page, our planet wouldn't even show up. Our sun would be a dot.

All this is enormous beyond our wildest imaginings. The nearest star to our sun, so my young people tell me, is Alpha Centauri. Yet even that star is so far away that any thought of earthperson's ever reaching it alive is totally beyond the ability of our present technology, and our galaxy is but one of many galaxies scattered through the expanding and apparently limitless reaches of space.

When we try to conceive of the enormity of the universe, it's enough to make one scream, "Stop! I want to get off! Give me that old-time religion, and a pox on all your solar systems and galaxies and families of galaxies and limitless space, and all that godless tommy rot! Carry me back to that old geocentric universe where I amounted to something!" The truth of the matter, however, is that the cosmology of Genesis was probably as vast a concept to the writer, who could only walk or ride up to twenty miles a day, as the twentieth century cosmology is to us, who can go around the earth in a day and are fast approaching interplanetary travel. The vaster the universe, the greater God's glory as its Creator, and thus the more profound the theological statements of Genesis.

The purpose of the creation stories is theological. Like the rest of the Bible, these accounts attempt to lead us to a knowledge of God and to an understanding of ourselves. They encourage us to a loving relationship with God and to a working-living relationship under Him.

CHAPTER 3

THE ROOTS OF DAWN

The literalist spirit bred or conditioned into us gets uncomfortable with this line of thought. If it's not <u>true</u> (by which we really mean <u>empirically accurate</u>), what's it doing in the Bible? Who thought up this view of the universe if it's not <u>right</u> (by which we really mean <u>empirically accurate</u>)? Good questions, both. Let's look at the second one first.

I believe that the view of the cosmos expressed in Genesis is the correct one. Let's compare apples with apples, however, or firmaments with firmaments as the case is here. Other peoples, way back then, also had views of the cosmos. Mosaic Yahwism (the religion of the One True God) grew up in a world that was already very old. The Babylonians and Egyptians had long since set down well-established and minutely detailed descriptions of the appearance and nature of the universe, and how it got that way. The Hebrew genius, growing out of this world, was innovative, in fact, nothing short of inspired.

In the barren sands and fetid marshes of southern Iraq today, are the nearly forgotten memories of Sumer. It was

Creation <u>Versus</u> Evolution? Not Really!

at Sumer, most archeologists agree, that the first writing
civilization began in about 3500 B.C. As the Sumerian Way
collapsed and arose phoenix-like from its own ashes in a
dozen different stages with a dozen different names down to
and beyond the time of Abraham, their seers thought, their
priests chanted, their scribes wrote. They thought and sang
and wrote about the appearance and the nature of the cosmos.
When we look at a cuneiform document called <u>Ennuma Elish</u>
(<u>When</u> <u>as</u> <u>Yet</u>), scholars who can read the thing tell us it
describes the origin of a sky-vaulted, geocentric universe
that is alive with the sound of "religion", violence and
agony.

According to one book about ancient mythologies, the
Babylonian Creation Epic can be summarized like this:[4]

> Water is the primordial element. <u>Apsu</u>,
> the "male principle", fresh water of the
> abyss encircling the (eventual) earth
> disk, is met by <u>Tiamat</u>, the "female prin-
> ciple", salt water. That meeting produces
> <u>Mummu</u>, creative chaos, tumult. This, in
> turn, leads to vaguely defined sea monsters
> named <u>Lakhmu</u> and <u>Lakhamu</u>, who somehow pro-
> duce a united sky-earth mountain called
> <u>An-Ki</u>.

Creation Versus Evolution? Not Really!

At this point, orderly diagramming becomes impossible. The story unfolds: Anshar and Kishar give birth to Anu ("the powerful"), Ea ("vast intellect"), and to other divine principles - the Igigi in the sky and the Anunnake on the earth and in the underworld.

Apsu and Tiamat take counsel to destroy their descendants because it's getting too noisy in the primeval oceanic-existence. Ea, the intellect, attempts to defuse this conspiracy. He captures Apsu and Mummu, but Tiamat, the salt water, eludes capture. She goes into a rage, calls up her auxiliaries, and the war is on! The coalition of her descendants is no match for her.

Enter Marduk! (From whence, God only knows; the ancients did not have to account for such things by logic). Winning the concession of dictatorial powers from the other gods should he be victorious, Marduk marches against the malevolent Tiamat with all the implements of war. He catches her in his net, sends a hurricane to distend her belly, fires his fatal arrow, and stands triumphant over her dead body.

After a mop-up action which consigns all of Tiamat's auxiliaries to the underworld, Marduk returns to the corpse of the late salt water goddess and splits her body lengthwise. Creative even under these sanguine circumstances, Marduk arches Tiamat's ventral half up, up and around, to create the sky vault. Her dorsal half becomes the earth below. The basic cosmos designed, he fills in the rest of the created order.

To keep the other gods happy, a species of slave is created and called mankind. Marduk fashions the first man out of a clot of blood from Kingu, Tiamat's defeated general.[5] After this, he fills in the remaining phenomena - the great rivers, vegetation and animals - by divine command.

A story like that is, as I say, next to impossible to illustrate. It just doesn't follow logically. While the

ancients were no dummies, their religious mythology was pre-
logical. It did not operate, nor was it told, in the "Greek"
way that you and I assume is normal, natural and universal.
Linear thought, cause and effect, consistency of a divine
character's sex, identity, personality, lineage and manifestation (the kind of logical approach with which we function)
they had not developed.

The basic parallel to the cosmology in Genesis 1 comes
through plainly, though the details are certainly different.
When all is said and done, the universe is composed of a
sky vault above, sealing out the potentially destructive
primal waters from the earth below the vault.

The noted Sumerologist, Samuel Noah Kramer, has written
a fascinating little book, History Begins at Sumer.   In it,
he traces the conception of the ancient cosmos even further
back than the Babylonian Creation Epic.6   The account is more
complete and less bloody than the Marduk/Tiamat story:

> First there was a primordial sea in chaos,
> the sea was not just water; it was Nammu,
> the primal mother-goddess. She deposits
> An-Ki, the mountain of heaven and earth.
> An and Ki give birth to Enlil, the atmos-
> phere or air. It is this Enlil (not the
> later Marduk) who is in charge of the
> details of further creation. Perhaps be-
> cause his creativity is being stifled at
> home, cramped as he is between his par-
> ents, Enlil decides to separate them. An
> moves away, taking the heavens with him,
> and in the process forms (becomes) the
> sky vault. Enlil moves in the opposite
> direction, taking his mother with him.
> With all this space between the folks
> now, Enlil is free to do his thing. He
> forms, procreates or commands into being
> the rest of the gods (who assume the
> form of various natural phenomena) and
> the rest of life: first the moon (the

god, Sin or Nanna); from the moon, Utu
(the sun), Inanna (Venus), and other
celestial phenomena. The four chief
deities (and components of the universe),
then, are: An (sky), Ki (earth), Enlil
(air), and Ninhursag (water). From their
various unions, designs, and counter-
designs, the rest of the universe comes
into existence. Eventually, says Kramer,
the Sumerians recognized about a hundred
subsidiary gods who were "patron saints"
or guiding spirits for all occupations,
talents, buildings, institutions, and
tools. As the Sumerian looked about to
consider his universe and to ponder the
nature, the "meaning", of it all, he
envisioned its basic design to be something like this:

MUMMU –
PRIMAL
OCEAN

AN — SKY GOD

UTU — SUN GOD

SIN –
MOON
GOD

ENLIL
GOD
OF
AIR • BREATH • WIND

INANNA –
VENUS
GODDESS

SUMUGAN – MOUNTAIN
KING

IN CARE OF
DUMUZI –
SHEPHERD GOD

SLAVES OF THE
GODS

KI
EARTH GODDESS

ENKI – WATER
GOD

GODS AND
GODDESSES

IN THE
NETHERWORLD

Creation <u>Versus</u> Evolution? Not Really!

The cosmos was alive with the sound of religion! Gods and goddesses everywhere!

It is this Sumerian cosmology that influenced the shape of the universe as it was assumed and accepted throughout the ancient near east. Certainly it is the one that formed the basic design of "what the world looks like" with which the Genesis writers worked.

Through the process of creative borrowing, the ancient Egyptians also wound up with a basically Sumerian cosmology. To give a thumbnail sketch of the Egyptian version of what-went-on, however, is next to impossible. Take the complexity, confusion and role-switching of the Sumerian accounts, then multiply by ten. That's about the degree of difficulty in trying to outline a cohesive creation story from ancient Egyptian religion. We can draw in the protagonists, thanks to the tomb and temple paintings of old Egypt.

A rough outline of the Egyptian cosmology shows the long, lean giantess, Nut, goddess of the sky, arching over all. Far below is Geb, her husband, lover and twin brother. His anguished or disgruntled position forms the contours of the earth. The middle-man, arching Nut's body up and around to form the sky vault, is Shu, god of air and wind. He is acting under orders from Ra, chief of the gods, to keep Nut and Geb separated. Sun, moon, stars, winds, clouds, animals, man, waters, and every other physical detail could be drawn in, each personified in another deity. Elsewhere, Nut is represented as the Cow of Heaven, with Shu holding her up, and with all the other gods and goddesses of the universe walking along beneath her.

The point is, again, that any way you draw it or de-scribe it, the ancients conceived of the universe as a sky vault over an earth-island, submerged in the primordial sea.

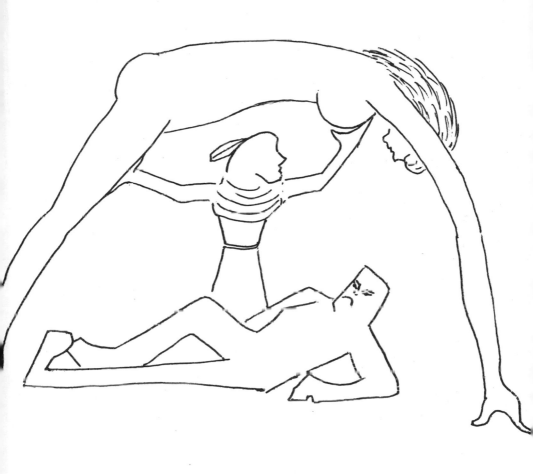

CHAPTER 4

THE GENIUS OF THE HEBREWS

So what's so special about the Genesis accounts? What's so different between the Bible's stories of creation and the stories of the surrounding cultures? The answer leaps off the page at you. Turn the page and look!

SUMER - EGYPT AND EVERYWHERE BETWEEN

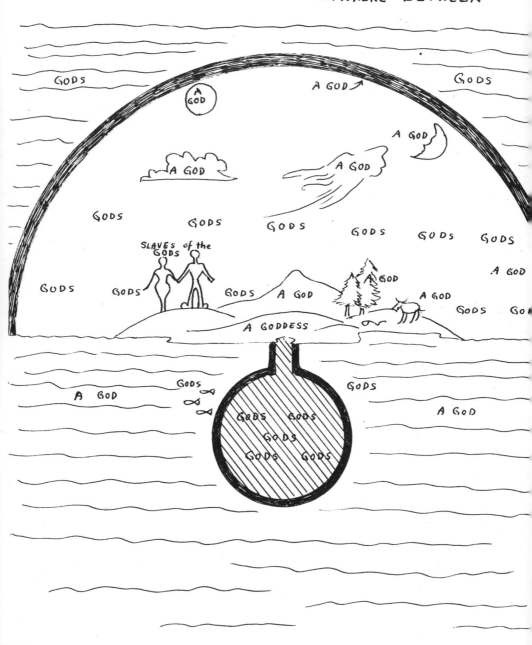

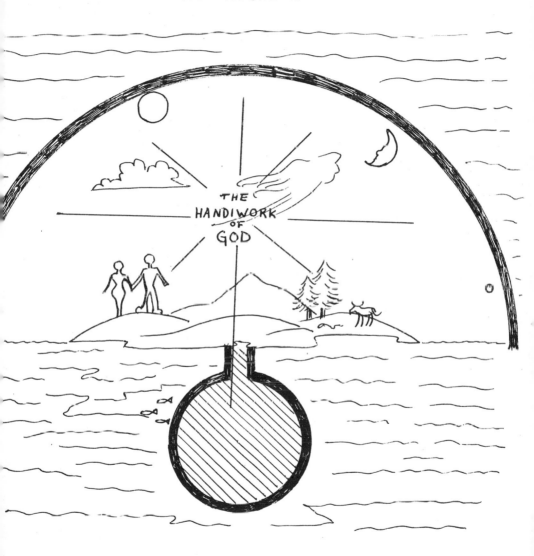

THE HANDIWORK OF GOD

Creation <u>Versus</u> Evolution? Not Really!

The Hebrew "genius" is in its revelation of God. Surrounded on every side by ancient cultures that said the entire universe was a kaleidoscopic manifestation of all the deities, the Hebrew said, "No." Surrounded on every side by ancient cultures that said the universe got the way it is because the gods (who are good and bad, moral and immoral, purposeful and capricious, benevolent and malevolent) plotted, pounded, fornicated and slaughtered it into that shape, the Hebrew said, "No."

Quite clearly, the Hebrews didn't argue about the physical details of the cosmos. Nothing was more irrelevant. Given an age before there was scientific methodology, given an age before there were adequate instruments to measure cosmological data, one physical scheme of the universe was as good as the next. The one at hand, the Sumerian scheme, was perfectly acceptable. Whatever the world looked like, God had made it. Whatever the precise details of the operation of the cosmos, it operated the way God had designed it to operate. Whatever the chronological order in which things came to be, they had come by God's design. Whatever the length of time in which things came, they had come on a schedule that pleased God. All of it was good. Indeed, it was very good. But <u>none</u> of it <u>was</u> God. It was all His handiwork. It was all the product of His creative will, power, and goodness.

The Hebrew saw God, the Creator, and the cosmos, His creation, as two entirely different "things". One could see God's <u>witness</u> to Himself in and through creation, but one could not look at any created thing and say, "Lo, here is God", or "Lo, here is a part of a god."

God is as He was then. He is neither any part of, nor the entirety of, natural phenomena. He is the totally Other Yet He is not restrained by distance from His creation. He can "come down" and relate to it. He can relate to humankind, with all the nearness of a father to his children, because He has specially created <u>this</u> animal to be the God-relatable being.

Isn't that marvelous? Doesn't it stagger the imagination down to our rational, logical, toenails? The Hebrew creation epics are literally worlds apart from all the other ancient near eastern accounts.

CHAPTER 5

SOME THOUGHTS ON "TRUTH"

The Word is true! The creation accounts are true!
Judging from empirical evidence, the Genesis description of
the cosmos is not accurate. But the point it makes is absolutely true! God is Creator and Preserver of all things.
Humankind is uniquely created for fellowship with God, for
fellowship with itself, and for "stewardship" over the
whole earth. These are theological truths about God and
humanity and their relationship. There is no way they can
be tested. They are outside the purview of scientific investigation.

Science is true! As far as its rational assessment of
empirical data can take us, science is true. Working with
its methods and instruments, working with the (Greek) assumption of cause and effect, it aims at descriptive accuracy: What is it? What does it look like? How does it
react? How did it get here? These questions, so far as
their answers can be measured, are outside the purview of
theology.

You see, we make difficulties for ourselves when we
try to make the Bible say what it was not designed to say

and is not equipped to answer. Likewise, we create our own difficulties when we try to make science say what it was not conceived to say and is not equipped to answer.

If my definition of "truth" is: whatever the Bible says about any subject whatsoever, taken with uncompromising literalness, then of course there cannot be any truth in scientific description of a great many other things. My definition of "truth" has pronounced the answer before I ask my question.

If by "truth" I mean: only those conclusions that are verifiable by processing empirical data according to currently accepted scientific methods, then, of course, most everything in the Bible is untrue. Not only creation, but also preservation, salvation, justification, sanctification, Baptism, the Eucharist, the Church as the Body of Christ, the incarnation, the crucifixion, the resurrection, the humanity and divinity of Christ, the Holy Spirit, and God Himself. By that definition of "truth", <u>everything</u> in the Bible is up for grabs, except the names and reigns of a few kings and a handful of geographical place names. Just as before, my definition of "truth" has decided my answer before I ask my question.

On the other hand, if we agree that theology and science have their separate and God-given purviews and approaches to "truth", then there is no dilemma. The two become complementary instead of antagonistic. We could diagram it like this:

THE BIBLE ON CREATION	SCIENCE ON ORIGINS
Shows	Shows
GOD IN HIS REVEALED CREATION	GOD'S PHYSICAL METHOD OF OPERATING HIS CREATION
PURVIEW: Revealed Truth Accepted Only Through Faith	PURVIEW: Working Knowledge Accepted Only By Testing Or Demonstration
TYPICAL QUESTIONS/AREAS BIBLE IS EQUIPPED TO ANSWER/SPEAK ON:	*TYPICAL QUESTIONS/AREAS SCIENCE IS EQUIPPED TO ANSWER/SPEAK ON:*
*The existence of God.	*The phenomenon of religion.
*God as Creator/Preserver.	*Description of natural phenomena.
*People as creatures of God.	*Description of human beings ana- tonically, psychologically.
*Purpose of people/life/world.	*Description of the cosmos.
*Destiny of humanity.	*The age of the earth.
Etc.	Etc.

Truth → Truth → THE TRUTH ← truth ← truth

Creation Versus Evolution? Not Really!

You see, the Bible and science have two totally different assumptions about how truth is to be approached,
different assumptions about which questions are "worth"
asking and answering. The two, therefore, present very
different sounding conclusions. Yet the two approaches
equip the modern Christian in his search for one truth.

At the risk of over-simplifying, we can say that the
Bible answers the great "who" and "why" mysteries; science
aims at answers to the "what" and "how" questions of physical life. Thus:

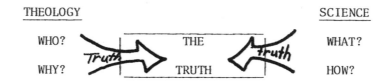

THEOLOGY		SCIENCE
WHO?	THE	WHAT?
WHY?	TRUTH	HOW?

Certainly that is over-simplifying. Anyone can compose
perfectly good theological questions beginning with what or
how. (What is God's will for me? How am I saved?) Likewise,
one can ask good scientific questions beginning with who and
why. (Who discovered the X-ray? Why does this chemical com-
bination react in this way?) The division of all truth into
these questions, then, is not rigid, but it does provide a
guideline.

Perhaps this next diagram better illustrates what I'm
talking about:

THEOLOGICAL QUESTIONS

I mean "WHO?" in the sense of
the "essence", the "nature",
the "individuality" - as in:

> "Who is God?"
> "Who is man?"

I mean "WHY?" in the sense of
"purpose" (not "function") -
as in:

> "Why am I here?"

(Not: "Why do I dream?")

And the reverse:

SCIENCE
DOES NOT ANSWER

THEOLOGY
DOES NOT ANSWER

SCIENTIFIC QUESTIONS

I mean "WHAT?" in the sense
of a thing's being described
or demonstrated according to
the instruments at hand - as
in:

> "What is the size/
> shape/age of the
> earth?"

And "HOW?" in the sense of
mechanics or functions - as in:

> "How do natural phe-
> nomena operate?"
> "How does it seem
> they got this way?"

Creation <u>Versus</u> Evolution? Not Really!

     The minute we force one approach to "truth" to carry the whole load, we're in trouble. Then the name-calling begins. Thus:

<table>
<tr><td></td><td>THE ONLY TRUTH</td><td>SCIENCE</td></tr>
<tr>
<td>

It is the purpose and purview of the Bible to answer all:

Who is God? Who is man? Why am I here? What is the age of the earth? How (mechanically) was the earth formed?
</td>
<td>

"TRUTH" defined as whatever is in accord with literal Bible statement ONLY

ERGO →
</td>
<td>

FALSE GODLESS (and probably) DAMNED SCIENCE
</td>
</tr>
</table>

Or the reverse:

BIBLE/RELIGION   THE ONLY TRUTH

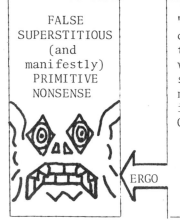

<table>
<tr>
<td>

FALSE SUPERSTITIOUS (and manifestly) PRIMITIVE NONSENSE
</td>
<td>

"TRUTH" defined as that which is verifiable by scientific methods and instruments ONLY

← ERGO
</td>
<td>

It is the purpose and purview of science to answer all:

Is there a God? Does man have a purpose? What is the apparent age of the earth? How (mechanically) does it seem the earth was formed?
</td>
</tr>
</table>

Both of these systems are unreal and unreasonable
things. The question is not Bible versus science at all.
These systems are hybrid monsters born of false fears:
biblicism and scientism. Neither the Bible nor science
presents itself as the total compendium of all knowledge
about the universe, nor as the only medium for grasping
all truth. It is biblicism or scientism that would do
that. It is between these two phantoms that most people
who ask the question, "What do you do with creation and
evolution?" feel themselves squeezed. It seems they have
to choose either one or the other. "Which one is true?"
The answer: neither. Not biblicism; not scientism. It
is both Bible and science, rightly approached and rightly
understood, that can help us gain the fulness of truth and
knowledge about ourselves and our universe.

A friend has suggested a helpful way to distinguish
between the truths of science and Bible, to ask the right
questions of each, and to see how each complements the
other:

> The dictionary gives two meanings for
> "truth": 1. fact, 2. transcendent,
> fundamental, spiritual reality. If
> you apply these two meanings to Bib-
> lical truth and scientific truth, you
> can arrive logically at the comple-
> mentary aspects of the two. Scientific
> truth is fact/accuracy, a sort of
> small "t" truth. It is specific truth,
> arrived at through applying ideas
> which are temporary (hypotheses), sub-
> ject to change as more data is
> uncovered, and developing into proba-
> bilities (theories). Biblical truth,
> on the other hand, is capital "T"
> Truth; it is fundamental reality,
> general, unchangeable, transcending
> specific fact. Small "t" truth is
> God's method of operation, the way
> in which He chooses to run things, or

> to make things self-running. Capital
> "T" Truth is God Himself, His nature,
> His essence, and our oneness with Him.
> The two together make "THE TRUTH",
> that is, <u>total</u> <u>knowledge</u> <u>about</u> <u>God</u> <u>and</u>
> <u>ourselves</u>, complete Truth, and are
> thus complementary.

"East is east and west is west", but the two <u>do</u> meet.
They meet as they help me to define and comprehend the center, the totality of life, where I stand. They may appear
to have differing answers. Understanding where each is
coming from as they give those answers, however, allows me -
indeed, allows us all - to grasp that fuller picture of the
universe and the place of people in it.

CHAPTER 6

ALTERNATIVES

The answer that works for me certainly will not work for everyone. To stand in the center and to reap the benefits of both "east" and "west", Bible and science, is simply not possible for many. The follower of biblicism will continue to force the Bible to pose as a scientific text book. The follower of scientism will continue vainly to pursue "the ultimate mysteries of the universe" in science, even when science is not going that route.

There are other possibilities however. Some of them seem perilously close to biblicism or scientism; some are philosophical reconciliations of Bible and science. In any case, they are alternatives that some persons may find more helpful as an answer to the question of this book.

THE ELASTIC "YOM"

Yom is the Hebrew word for "day". God created the world, says the Genesis 1 account, in six days and rested on the seventh day. In every class where we've discussed creation and evolution, invariably some student is quick to point out, "Yes, but it doesn't say how long each of those days was. They might not have been twenty-four hour days like ours. If those 'days' were much, much longer than the ones we know, then there's room for evolution within the limits of the Biblical account!"

"Yes," adds another student, "the Bible says somewhere, 'with the Lord one day is as a thousand years!' Why not millions of years?"

Certainly this is a direction that works not only for some students I have known, but for many Christians of all ages as well. For me, however, the Elastic Yom raises as many problems as it answers.

"But do not ignore this one fact, beloved, that with the Lord one day is as a thousand years, and a thousand years as one day." (2 Peter 3:8) The holy writer penned that line as a part of his encouragement to keep the faith in the face of scoffers. The end of the world was coming in all the deliberate speed of God's good time. Believers, then, should not think God slow in staging the cosmic de-nouement, Judgment Day, but rather trust that He is in control of all events and all times.

Somewhere along the line, a sub-school of pious thought has developed which applies this verse, rather out of con-text, to the question of creation and evolution. Since man's time and God's time are different, those first days could really have been millenia, eons, ages, not just twenty-four hour days. By this reasoning, Bible and science are really saying the same thing; they're just expressing it in dif-ferent words. My problems with the Elastic Yom are these:

1. The <u>a priori</u> assumptions of the Elastic Yom seem to be: a) that the truthfulness of the Bible is dependent upon its <u>accuracy</u> in accounting for the origin of earth and mankind; b) that science has proven that it took billions of years to get from first explosion to present life; and, therefore, c) that the two <u>have to be</u> harmonized. However

contrived, however much Bible and science may kick
and scream at being forced into clothes not designed for them, the two must be made to say the
same thing. It is good "reason". Truth is one;
therefore, it should say the same thing, no matter
how you approach it. Good reason; but not necessarily good Bible study or good science.

2. When the Hebrew writer said, "day", he meant day.
   The evening and the morning, the succession of
   darkness and daylight as we know it, was the first
   day, the second, and all the others.

3. If each day is stretched into an eon, and if you
   leave the textual succession of darkness and daylight intact, you have a most unlikely epic.
   First, an unpleasant, eons-long night would freeze
   the earth into solid ice caps, then an equally unpleasant, eons-long day would fry it to a crisp.
   That this should happen seven times in succession
   would not be much of a program for the development
   and sustaining of life as we know it.

4. The Elastic Yom does not address the "problem" of
   the description of what the world looks like according to Genesis 1. However long those creative
   days were, Bible and science simply will not jibe
   on cosmology.

THE MATURE CREATION

If one demands that the Bible and science be reconciled,
the Mature Creation seems a promising alternative. It ac-
cepts the premise that science is working in good faith,
using the best principles and instruments of scientific
method. When all the data are assessed and an age for the
earth is suggested, science has proceeded fairly and accurately. This thing really is 10,000 years old, according
to scientific measurement. That thing really is a million
years old in the same way. It's not that the instruments

or methods are faulty. It's just that God made them to have those apparent ages. Really, the whole creation is only ten or twenty thousand years old - or maybe only six thousand, as Bishop Ussher calculated.

Via time machine, we go back a few thousand years to Adam in the garden. As we stand there, somewhat embarrassed that he is not embarrassed at his lack of clothing, we remark on the natural wonders at hand:

"What a magnificent redwood! It must be 5000 years old!"

"Oh no. It's only two hours old. God put it there just this morning."

If we were to cut down that tree and count the rings, it might indeed have 5000 rings. By scientific method, the age of the tree would be 5000 years by every test, but science could not measure the fact that it was only just created. Created mature. Voila! The twain are reconciled! Bible and science propose different answers apparently, but that's only because science is bound by instruments and methods that lead it, in all good faith, to erroneous conclusions.

In the same way, dinosaur bones are real; it's just that dinosaurs themselves didn't really live! Their apparent remains were simply created where and as we find them in the fossil beds. The petroleum pools all over the world appear to be the results of eons of matter decayed. Really they were created that way, a few thousand years back.

Name any "problem" from Kenya man to cave paintings. No case. They were created that way. As a reconciliation of Bible and science, the Mature Creation alternative is beyond reproach.

I fault it on two counts, however. In the first place, it still does not reconcile the cosmology of Genesis 1 (sky vault, earth island, etc.) with currently verifiable understandings of the shape and scope of the universe.

Secondly, the Mature Creation is theologically suspicious. God is cast in the role either of Cosmic Bungler or Celestial Prankster. Thus: As we time-warp back into the first six days and look over the "shoulder" of the Great Bungler, we hear Him say, "Rats! I said, 'horses!' And I mean horses! Whatever these are, let them be buried!" (Exeunt apparently prehistoric monsters.) "That's not a tiger! I meant something with stripes! Besides, those eye teeth are ridiculous. Bury that thing!" (Exeunt the great cats.) That sort of indecision and second-thoughting doesn't match up with the theological account of a God who commanded, and it was done. Nor does that kind of abrupt displeasure with things created match up with the theological account of a God who viewed everything and called it good.

As the Celestial Prankster, God would be saying, "Let's see how Darwin explains this!" Or, "(Chuckle) Won't Leakey get a kick out of this?" If you grant, however, that God has a sense of humor (after all, He created you and me, didn't He?), then the Mature Creation alternative can be viewed as reasonable. It allows you to have one truth If you don't press the details of the first account too closely, you may believe the Bible's presentation of events as factually accurate and still pursue a scientific career. You just have to keep remembering in that career that your scientific measurements of time, age, and many other things aren't really real. They only seem to be.

It is an answer that truly works for many.

THE FLOOD DID IT

"More things were wrought by flood than this world dreams of." In the mouth of a Taoist, that borders on the profound. In the mouth of a Bible scholar, it does not.

Creation <u>Versus</u> Evolution? Not Really!

The beautiful thing about the Flood alternative is
that, superficially, it appears to resolve any difficulty
in matching up the Genesis accounts with geography and
cosmology as we know them, or with the ages of strata as
geologists guess them.

Thus: Why can't you draw a map of the four rivers
branching off the one flowing out of Eden? (See page 53.)
Elementary! The flood did it! The flood wiped out every
trace of Eden, raised mountains, lowered valleys, rerouted
rivers, filled the seas, etc.

Why do the fossil beds and petroleum deposits of pre-
sumably prehistoric life appear in the strata they do?
Simple. The flood did it. Too big for the ark, they were.
A case of planned obsolescence from the start.

Why does it appear some mountains used to be below sea
level or that some deserts were once humid tropical jungles?
What else? The flood did it. It carried those clam shells
right up the mountain sides, then left them high and dry.
It swirled that tropical vegetation around to all sorts of
new locations.

What about that sky vault in Genesis 1? What indeed!
The flood eroded it away. All that water, you know. Firmaments are only so firm. The waters that used to be held
in check by the firmament are now the seas and the atmos-
phere below.

The difficulty in embracing this "Flood Did It" expla-
nation for every left-over problem is that it ignores the
present tense of the Biblical accounts. The holy writers
were describing the universe as they knew it from simple,
land-bound observation in the pre-Ptolemaic age. "God made
that firmament; and it's still there, as any fool can see!"
The firmament is there not only in pre-flood Genesis, but
also in post-flood Psalms, Proverbs, Job, etc. (Significant-
ly, it is <u>not</u> there anymore in the New Testament. These
writers work instead with a hellenistic assumption of heav-
enly spheres surrounding a global earth - third heaven,

seventh heaven, principalities, powers, dominions, degrees of glory, etc.) What applies to the firmament is true of those four rivers flowing out of Eden. In Genesis 1 the writer speaks of them in the present tense: "These are the names of the rivers out of Eden; they are still flowing around this and that area, according to reliable reports from those parts."

"The Flood Did It" is a variation of a basic biblicistic concern: If the cosmology isn't scientifically verifiable, maybe the theology isn't "true" either. The truthfulness of the Bible becomes dependent, then, on man's ability to account for and explain away any "discrepancy" between the Bible's account and scientific data. The poor flood gets deluged with the overwhelming responsibility of bailing God, or the Bible, out of the imagined difficulties. God and the Bible don't need that kind of protection. There was a flood. It must have had a profound effect on geography, but it does not neatly answer every query or dispose of every geological theory.

THEY BORROWED FROM US

What about all those alleged parallels with literature more ancient than the Biblical accounts as we have them? What about <u>Ennuma Elish</u>, <u>Gilgamish</u>, the Cow of Heaven, and all that pagan tommy rot? Some would insist, "Why they borrowed from us, not we from them!"

According to this line of reasoning, the six day creation account was handed down by God Himself. Adam received it and passed it on to Seth. Seth passed it on...eventually to Abraham. On down it came into that comparatively recent time when it was recorded as we have it. The account came down accurately only in Israel's religious history. Any alleged parallels between Genesis and the records of other cultures were due simply to a garbled transmission of the true account as it reached those other lands.

Creation <u>Versus</u> Evolution? Not Really!

As a contrivance, "They Borrowed From Us" seems rea-
sonably unassailable, but holding to this school <u>does</u>
require belief in inspired oral tradition or notebook-
keeping as an article of faith. Empirically speaking, the
religious records and accounts of those other cultures were
written down earlier than ours. It's just that they wrote
down the wrong thing.

There are problems with this, however. The first is
that there seems to have been another, equally authoritative
tradition or notebook handed down. As we noted at length
earlier, the second creation account (Genesis 2:4b on) is
different from the first in significant detail. If the
nature of Biblical truth is its accuracy in describing the
methods and stages of the origins of things and of mankind,
then we are left with an unresolvable difficulty: two
unique accounts, two absolutely authoritative sources. If
the nature of Biblical truth is something else, only then
does this marked difference in detail cease to matter.

Secondly, if the flow of ideas, institutions and in-
ventions in the ancient near east seems to have been from
Sumer outwards (to Babylon, to Assyria, to Syria, to Phoe-
nicia, etc.), is it scholarship or piety to maintain that
in this one case the flow was from the desert (wandering
Arameans) into sedentary Sumer? If Abraham (about 1800 B.C.)
or Moses (about 1250 B.C.) had the "right" perspective,
could this really influence a cosmology that already pre-
dated them by a thousand years in one case and by nearly
two thousand in the other?

Again, the whole approach raises more unlikelies than
it answers. Plausible as it is for some people, it seems
a contrived leap of faith in the direction of biblicism.
From any other point of view (good archeology, good scholarship, good sense, or Biblical Christianity) it seems either
indefensible or needless.

CREATION RESEARCH

With the preceeding alternatives (The Elastic Yom, The Mature Creation, The Flood Did It, They Borrowed From Us), it may be that I have misrepresented ideas or approaches that some would find of more help than mine in reaching a personal, workable, reconciliation between Bible and science. In truth, there are dedicated Christians who would find my answer unworkable for them. If it's in the Bible, they reason, it's got to be true scientifically as well as theologically. With enough research, they maintain, the Bible's creation accounts can be shown to be empirically valid.

You should be aware, then, of the existence and work of the Creation Research Society. The society is composed of Christian men and women, some with impressive credentials in certain areas of scientific endeavor. They are convinced that the Bible's straight-forward presentation of the Creation, the Deluge, etc., is defensible scientifically. To present their point of view, they support research expeditions to distant points (as, for example, in search of Noah's ark), publish pamphlets and booklets favoring a literal reading of Genesis, and provide speakers for any group willing to listen.

In view of my "argument" that the Bible is a theological document that neither requires nor admits of scientific verification, I personally find the "cause" of the Society tedious and unnecessarily consuming of Christian time and talent. But you must make your own judgment. The Creation Research Society does provide many Christians with a meaningful solution to the apparent conflict between creation and evolution.

AUGUSTINIAN POTENTIALITY

Augustine was the bishop of Hippo, in what today is Tunisia. He died in the year A.D. 430 and left behind an interpretation of the faith that dominated Western Christianity for a thousand years.

Creation <u>Versus</u> Evolution? Not Really!

Augustine was neither a biblicist nor a scientist.
That these two approaches should attempt to resolve anything would have been, for him, absurd and irrelevant. For
him the difficulty was Biblical Christianity and Greek
Philosophy, in this case, Neo-Platonism. Creation was not
a doctrine to be proven scientifically. As with all other
doctrines, one had to come to grips with creation philo-
sophically. He wrestled with the written Word and philosophical constructs of his time, not to harmonize them but
to understand them.

For Augustine, creation did not happen in time at all.
It happened <u>in the beginning</u>. Time itself is a creation.
Thus, the six day account is not a literal description, but
the epic presentation of what happened in an instant - in
the beginning. All the world has existed at all times.
There never was a time when the world was not, since time
is a construct depending on the rotation of the earth.
"Time" before creation was not time at all, but God's time-
lessness - eternity.

As his ideas relate to the subject of this book, Augustine maintained that the world began to exist in the
beginning, but that not all things at the beginning of time
were as they are today. In that first instant of time, God
created everything, but everything did not show up at once.
Some things were created <u>in potential</u>. Though they had always existed as hidden "seeds", or as potentialities of
their eventual forms, many things did not actually appear
as a part of the created order until their time came. Thus,
to use our own examples, dairy cows have always existed.
They just didn't appear until more recently. Bulldogs and
dachshunds have been created since the beginning of time;
they simply didn't show up until much later. Enugus were
created in that same instant, they just...what's an enugu?
It hasn't shown up yet. It's time is not until later, long
after this generation has died and gone to heaven. In the
same way, for Augustine, people always were; they were
created in the beginning. It's just that they didn't appear
until much further down the line. Their potentiality was
always there. Their actuality, their form, their appearance, "happened" in due time.

You and I do not think much in terms of Augustine's
constructs anymore, but it's mind-boggling to realize that
one of the ancient church fathers came up with theistic
evolution 1400 years before Darwin ever saw the Galapagos
Islands. Augustine's point of departure was different
from ours. His statement of problem and acceptable evidence
was different, but in his wrestling with creation-in-poten-
tial, he placed a prophetic finger on the pulse of the
twentieth century.

THE INTERVENTION

Some of our Roman Catholic friends have an interesting
alternative about the origin of man: divine intervention
at some unspecified point in the creative/evolutionary
process. Since Thomistic philosophy is a basic guide for
understanding Roman theology and integrating it with the
world-as-we-know-it, the protestant dilemma (biblicism/
scientism) does not apply in Catholic circles. Neither
biblicism nor scientism is to be feared. One is relative-
ly free to operate with the better aspects of both of them,
without miring down in the dubious waters of either.

Though the New Baltimore Catechism is no longer offi-
cial in the Roman Catholic Church, it is instructive to our
study to look at a passage from it:

> a) The theory of evolution which teaches
> that higher forms of life developed from
> lower forms has offered no convincing,
> scientific proof that the human body de-
> veloped gradually from that of a lower
> animal.
>
> b) If scientific proof of such a develop-
> ment of the body of man could be had, it
> would not be opposed to Catholic doctrine
> provided that some special action of God
> is admitted not only in the creation of
> the soul but also in the production of
> the body of Adam.[7]

Creation <u>Versus</u> Evolution? Not Really!

There follow third and fourth subdivisions in this
section, but it's particularly the thought in a) and b)
that comes across so attractively. In a) the catechism
committee rightly observed that evolution is a good theory
in the scientific world. They simply ask that science be
honest to its own job description and not give out the im-
pression that evolution from one species to another has
been proven conclusively.

In b) the Roman Church served notice that, come what
may, she was prepared to deal with and envelop it all. Even
if evolution could be proved conclusively, it still wouldn't
destroy the faith, still wouldn't bring a particle of it
into doubt. The fact of evolution would not be a demonstration contrary to Roman doctrine. Man's uniqueness as a
physical and spiritual work of God would not be endangered.
When all the proofs were said and done, that uniqueness of
man would still be an unprovable or non-demonstrable article of faith, not a datum that even admits of scientific
investigation.

Here is an institutional church embracing the possibilities of a wider view of man's origin without selling
out and without being afraid. Too often we assume Rome's
attitude toward intellectual inquiry ended with the Gali-
leo story, and her attitude toward the Bible with the
Reformation. To be sure, from a protestant point of view,
our Roman friends still operate with a lot of pat answers
and blanket prohibitions, but the day of the chained Bible
and the chained scientist is past. It would be a good
thing to keep in mind when we talk about church history
around the end of October.

OMEGA POINT

Speaking of discipline in the Roman Church, we should
mention The Phenomenon of Man, a profound book by the late
Pére Teilhard de Chardin. This book, like all Chardin's
important works, could not be published during that writer's
lifetime. The Roman Church of that day considered its con-
tents potentially disturbing to the faith. Chardin was a

recognized paleontologist and philosopher, but he was also
an obedient Jesuit. He obeyed the order not to publish.
Truth is truth, whether it's published or not, he recognized.
If one had seen a new insight, many others would see the
same thing in short order. Meanwhile, not to worry. Since
his death in the mid-fifties, Chardin's works have enjoyed
a progressively wide circulation both inside and outside
the Roman Church, perhaps as he knew they would.

To summarize within the scope of this book, Chardin's
contribution was the statement that there is no real war
between science and the Bible, only a limitation of vision.
Everything has quality as well as quantity. When science
describes things only in quantities, it forgets the real
world of qualities. When religion describes things only in
qualities, it sometimes pretends the equally real world of
quantities doesn't exist. Everything from man to a stone
has both a "within" and a "without".

Chardin saw no problem in treating creation and preservation in terms of evolution. We came from somewhere, as
the expression of God's creative Word. We are going to
somewhere - to Omega Point - to reunion with God. He thought
it perfectly obvious and non-disturbing that, at some point
in the ordained evolutionary process, thinking man swarmed
into existence. We did not arrive full-blown, however, nor
have we yet achieved our destiny and potential. Thinking
man is still becoming, still growing into being, still
heading toward Omega Point. We are accustomed to thinking
that we have arrived. It is too unflattering to our self-
image to think of ourselves as merely links in a great
human chain that is heading someplace, but isn't there yet.
For Chardin, however, that's where it's at, and we with it:
growing in knowledge, growing in love, growing in communal-
ity (instead of individuality), on and on toward Omega
Point.

I recommend that you buy Chardin's book and read it
for yourself.[8] It is truly a mind-expanding experience.
Take some, leave the rest. You will be richer for the de-
tour. His is an alternative presentation that works for
many.

Creation <u>Versus</u> Evolution? Not Really!

BEYOND THE OUTER LIMITS

   This book would be incomplete without reference to the
works of Erich von Däniken.[9] The Swiss writer's thesis is
that the ancient records, whether Genesis or the Vedas,
should be taken literally. They are in fact, he maintains,
the accounts of visitors from outer space who "created" man
in their image. Landing their spaceships at an interstellar
pad in south Peru and at other places, they explored the
primitive life forms on this planet. Taking kindly to
proto-anthropos, they altered his genetic make-up to produce,
abruptly, <u>thinking man</u>! They instructed him in the way he
should go. With a spot-check system of occasional visits,
they monitored his further progress.

   The evidence for all this, von Däniken avers, includes
various unexplainable architectural phenomena, rock paintings of spaceships and space-suited humanoids, and ancient
accounts by the first writers about a race of gods in
spaceships, either fighting among themselves or programming
humankind.

   The earth itself and its life forms happened, presumably, by an evolutionary process. But thinking humankind
was a deliberate mutation produced in the laboratories of
the spacepeople. As these visitors were so vastly advanced
intellectually and technologically over their "creation",
they were remembered as "gods" by succeeding generations.

   Well, what does one say? I <u>am</u> an American; I <u>love</u> a
good science fiction thriller; von Däniken's hypothesis <u>is</u>
fascinating. I have at least three very dear friends who
get upset with me for not taking von Däniken much more se-
riously than I do. For them, his thesis is demonstrably
valid, while my reservations seem needlessly institutional-
ized or reactionary. I must allow for the possibility that
they are right. (I should also tell you, I am an avid "von
Däniken watcher". I have read his books, seen his movie,
and attended one of his personal appearances.) While I am
always fascinated by von Däniken's presentation of his
ideas, I have problems with his evidence.

My first concern is his unequal use of source material.
If a literal reading of a passage from the ancients seems to
substantiate his case, then that section should be taken
"religiously". The passages that don't fit don't count.
They must have been added by people who hadn't seen the
"gods". For readers who are only slightly acquainted with
the Gilgamish Epic, the Old Testament, and the Vedas, von
Däniken's thesis seems marvelously convincing. To read in
toto the ancient documents is not necessarily to come to his
conclusions at all. Von Däniken excuses himself in this un-
even use of his "sources" with the demurrer that he is a
self-made self-taught man; he is not obligated to proceed by
methods that others have defined as scholarly. He is simply
asking questions and suggesting the shape of answers.

A second difficulty I have with von Däniken's evidence
is his badgering of the witnesses. As I read it, he repeatedly attempts to have people admit, "Yes! Yes! These
things were put here by superior intelligences from outer
space!" When they refuse to talk, or attempt to give him
answers other than the ones he wants, they are obviously
trying to keep the cosmic secrets of extraterrestrial gods
safe from the civilized world. In interviews with other
worthies, if a chance remark would seem to lend credence to
his hypothesis, that remark is pounced upon. All the alternative suggestions in the rest of the interview are
simply disregarded.

A third difficulty is the absoluteness with which von
Däniken interprets the alleged artifacts of the alleged
space-visitors. Take this rock painting! Obviously it's a
primitive attempt to represent a being in a close-fitting
space suit! Or this! Obviously a statue of a humanoid
wearing goggles! Or this! Obviously a superior intelligence at the controls of a spaceship! It seems any stray
line becomes a rocket exhaust or the path of a space flota-
tion; any humanoid in any garb becomes a visitor from outer
space. It is certainly plausible that these artifacts could
admit of these interpretations. It is equally plausible to
interpret them otherwise, as archeologists have long been
doing.

Creation <u>Versus</u> Evolution? Not Really!

Though von Däniken's thesis and assessment of the evidence do not "work" for me personally, it is important (and only fair) to remember that in my own lifetime rocket ships, Buck Rogers, laboratory mutations, and atomic destruction have all moved from the category of far-out science fiction to the category of commonplace reality. That alone is enough to give one pause before a too-easy dismissal of von Däniken's basic ideas.

OTHERS

Like the Athenians, with their pedestal dedicated to the unknown god, it seems good sense to leave a space for the alternatives I have not covered, because I don't even know about them. There must be shelves full of other works by individuals who have wrestled through to their answers to the question, "What do you do with creation and evolution?" As the recent appearance of von Däniken's works remind us, there must be shelves yet to come. To you, I commend the past and future wrestlers, as far as your question extends and until your need is met.

In any case, I have given you the answer that works for me, and also those of biblicism, scientism, sub-schools somewhere in between, philosophical interpretations, and other possibilities, so far as I'm aware of them. I hope there are directions in all these possibilities that help you to formulate the answer that works for you.

CHAPTER 7

LOOSE ENDS AND NEW QUESTIONS

In presenting this answer that works for me, there are at least three questions I have not dealt with. It may be that one or all three of them dangle as loose ends in making my answer helpful for you. The questions:

If any of this answer is correct, then when did people get their souls?

It any of this answer is correct, then how did human-kind fall into sin?

If any of this answer is correct, then why didn't any-one ever tell me these things before?

I have a beautiful answer for the third question. Let me be honest and say, for the first two, I honestly don't know. Then let me explain why I don't know.

THE SOUL

In a sense, the origin of the human soul is irrelevant to the scope of this book. It would be best handled in a separate and longer study. I say that, not because I don't want to deal with the subject, but because Genesis doesn't deal with it. Again, it's a matter of being honest with the text itself.

The account in Genesis 1 (verses 26, 27) speaks of humankind as being created in the "image of God", "after our likeness". It can be argued that the holy writer had in mind physical likeness when he wrote that line. On the other hand, the fact that God created male <u>and</u> female in His image and after His likeness points more probably to the idea of some spiritual quality. This quality is nowhere defined or elaborated upon in the surrounding verses. It is linked to the charge to humankind to be viceroy, "fill the earth and subdue it; and have dominion over" all the other animals (verse 28), but exactly what the likeness is to God is not discussed.

The catechism I grew up with defined the image of God as the "righteousness and true holiness" that humanity had before the fall, but not after. Vestigial remnants of the image of God, I was told, might be such uniquely human characteristics as intelligence, self-awareness, the ability to worship, and the idea of eternity. That may be. It is not, however, evident on the basis of this particular text.

In other biblical texts, humanity, existing in the image of God and under the divine charge to be viceroy, appears to be in healthy condition long after the fall. Thus, for example, Psalm 8:5-6:

> Yet thou hast made him little less than
> God, and dost crown him with glory and
> honor.

> Thou hast given him dominion over the
> works of thy hands; thou hast put all
> things under his feet.

Is this "image" or "likeness" the same thing we mean by "soul"? Or is it a characteristic, an ability, a capacity? The text does not actually say.

The account in Genesis 2 (verse 7) says, God "breathed
into his nostrils the breath of life; and man became a living being." The King James Version says, "living soul."
The Hebrew word translated in either case is nephesh, which,
strictly speaking, is not "soul". Though it is nowhere
neatly defined in the Old Testament, nephesh is related to
the drawing of breath from God and the flowing of blood. It
is "life principle", with very physical manifestations.

Thus, in the covenant with Noah following the flood, God
allows mankind to eat any moving thing in the animal world,
"only you shall not eat the flesh with its life, that is,
its blood." (Genesis 9:5) The blood of people shall not be
shed for any reason, "for God made man in his own image."
(Genesis 9:6) Something about the blood belongs only to
God; it is a part or a manifestation of an indefinable "life
principle". Breath is the other part. God breathed into
Adam's nostrils and he became a living being, but elsewhere
(Psalm 104:29-30) the same divine breath creates and sustains animals:

> ...when thou takest away their breath,
> they die and return to their dust.
>
> When thou sendest forth thy Spirit
> [breath, margin] they are created.

Whatever nephesh is, it is something man has in common
with the animal kingdom. You can make a good, textual, case
that the blood/breath/life principle of people is "higher",
more special, than that of the beasts. It still does not
tell us much about the origin or description of the soul.

Not counting the popular or colloquial derivatives,
one dictionary defines "soul" as:

1. an entity which is regarded as the immortal or
   spiritual part of the person and, though having no
   physical or material reality, is credited with the

functions of thinking and willing, and hence deter-
mining all behavior.
2. the moral or emotional nature of man.

3. spiritual or emotional warmth, force...

4. vital or essential part, quality, or principle...

8. the spirit of a dead person, thought of as separate
from the body and leading an existence of its own.

Notice that very little of a definition like this re-
lates to the Hebrew assertion that there is a divine principle or mystery at the root of all breath and blood. Our
definition of "soul" comes chiefly from the Greek assumption
that "the <u>real</u> me" is spiritual, not physical. Rather than
being a totality (flesh and non-flesh at the same time),
"the <u>real</u> me" sort of lives in this body for a while; then,
when the body ceases to function, "the <u>real</u> me" flies free
and immortal to wherever spirits go.

To read this Greek kind of soul-talk back into the accounts of Genesis is dubious procedure indeed. The patri-
archs and prophets simply did not conceive of humankind's
God-relatable quality in this way. You and I are much more
at home with the "soul" concept assumed by later Old Testament writers and by some of the New Testament writers because they wrote in the setting of that Greek culture which,
to a large extent, has defined our idea of "soul".

Mark Twain once remarked, "Man is the foremost of God's
creatures. Who found that out?" What Twain asked as an ag-
nostic, the wisdom writer mulled over as a seeker after
divine truth:

...The fate of the sons of men and the
fate of beasts is the same; as one dies,
so dies the other. They all have the
same breath, and man has no advantage
over the beasts; for all is vanity.
All go to one place; all are from the

> dust, and all turn to dust again. Who
> knows whether the spirit of man goes
> upward and the spirit of the beast goes
> down to the earth?

Ecclesiastes 3:19-21

The Greek concept of "soul" probably is accepted more widely among Christians today than it was accepted or held among the writers of the New Testament. Test this by asking your acquaintances about life after death. I believe the responses will indicate more conviction about the immortality of the soul than about the resurrection of the body. In the Apostles' Creed and the Nicene Creed, however, we affirm the resurrection as an article of faith and do not allude to the soul, immortal or otherwise. In the New Testament, likewise, emphasis is not on the salvation of one's immortal soul; it is on the resurrection of one's redeemed body (or total person). The eschatological (last times; Judgment Day) teachings and, certainly, the resurrection and ascension narratives of the four Gospels assume the late Hebrew understanding of the resurrection of the body. In Paul's letters (e.g. 1 Corinthians 15, 1 Thessalonians 4:13-18) "immortality" applies not to a disembodied soul but to the "glorified body" of the believer, resurrected on the last day.

Having said all of this, the question is still valid. "When did we get a soul?" The question is valid because, however we define the soul, most of us work with some idea of an inner, unique, God-relatable, quality or entity. Whether we lean more in the direction of "self-awareness - the capacity for contemplation", or more toward "the little ghost with wings" that we see in cartoons, we insist that we recognize as a reality an indefinable "something" we call the soul. Image of God, nephesh, soul, how did we get it?

I don't know.

If people as we know them today are the only earth creatures who ever had souls, some kind of divine intervention in the rather recent past (say, within the last 10,000

Creation <u>Versus</u> Evolution? Not really!

to 50,000 years) might be necessary as an article of faith.
The writers of the <u>New Baltimore Catechism</u> suggested this
(see page 99 above). If this intervention was timed to ex-
clude those humanoids categorized as Cro Magnon, then, presumably, only homo sapiens will inherit the Kingdom.

Personally, I lean more in the direction of Chardin's
(philosophical) hypothesis, that everything that exists has
"soul" as well as "body". St. Paul is on this "wave length"
when he says (Romans 8:19-23) that the whole creation, not
only Christian people, eagerly longs and groans in travail
for the fulfillment of God's grand design. The writer of
Ecclesiastes observed with total disenchantment that whatever our fate, beasts and people were in the same boat. St.
Paul rejoiced about it; whatever our fate, God's design
for the universe is bigger than all of us! Perhaps the most
profound statement of this truth was that of St. Francis of
Assisi. He simply went and evangelized the birds and the
Muslims.

We could maintain, with Augustine, that as humanity
has always been (even if only in potential), so at all times
the soul has always been. It simply may not have "appeared"
until its designated time. Does this mean that Neanderthal
man or Kenya man went to heaven? Or will go to heaven? I
don't know. If you are working with the probabilities 1)
that man evolved to his present form, and 2) that man today
has a soul, then your answer to that question depends on
your speculations about other questions:

1. Has "soul" developed in direct ratio to other human
   developments (e.g. cognitive ability, self-awareness,
   intelligence)? I may think it has, but I don't know;
   there is no way to prove it.

2. Is it a certain "level" or "amount" of soul that
   qualifies one as human? If so, which proto-man had
   what level of soul? How can it be proved?

3. Does heaven depend on humanity's having a soul or
   does it depend, as the New Testament writers affirm,

on the grace of God in Jesus Christ? If the latter,
then what prohibits God from saving anyone and anything, living or dead, present or pre-historic?

The entire line of questioning becomes so speculative
that any answer will do, this side of the grave. It honestly will. We won't know as we are known until a later date.
Meanwhile, if I read Paul rightly in Romans 8, I'm betting
that the whole shooting match is heading God's way, whether
it knows it or not.

THE FALL

If any of this answer is correct, then how did humankind fall into sin? That is, if Genesis 2 was not intended
to be a factual account of the manner and method in which
all creation actually occurred, then what becomes of the
fall narrative in Genesis 3, written by the same school?
If humanity did not fall into sin, why do we need a Savior?
What becomes of Christianity itself?

Here again, the scope of the question is honestly a
whole separate book. Our theological assumptions certainly are interrelated. You can't touch one facet without a
"ripple effect" that makes you see larger areas to explore,
other circles to ponder.

Like the creation accounts, the fall narrative has its
roots in that same ancient Sumerian religious literature.
There are two sources I can suggest to you for vigorous exploration of the subject. One is a small booklet by Dr.
Norman Habel[10], the other is Volume One of The Interpreter's
Bible[11]. The two of these will point you to many other
sources and authors and will give you a variety of current
scholarly opinions and "accepted" understandings about the
fall narrative. (Be assured, this inquiry will only cause
that "ripple effect" to continue. To find satisfactory
answers and directions about the fall will only whet your
appetite for the exploration of other areas of religious
inquiry. All this can only be to the good! Keep inquiring!)

Creation <u>Versus</u> Evolution? Not Really!

None of this detracts from the importance of the question, "If any of this is correct, is humanity fallen or not? Do we need a Savior or not?" My answer to both questions is, yes. "Yes, I need help in 'getting my act together' with both God and my fellow human beings; yes, Jesus is the answer." I can't prove either assertion with empirical evidence. They are both statements of faith. It is important to note that a literal reading of the Biblical narrative does not <u>prove</u> either of these things.

The Bible speaks from faith to faith. That's why I have said throughout this book, the Bible is a theological document, not a scientific textbook. My brother, the biblicist, cannot <u>prove</u> the fall or salvation in a scientific way. He can <u>cite</u> chapter and verse where these truths are recorded, and then <u>choose to interpret</u> the entirety of the report as literally <u>factual</u>. Meanwhile, I, his brother, can look at the same passages and accept the <u>truths</u> asserted therein without necessarily feeling bound to believe that this or that event happened in exactly this way. In other words, it does not destroy my faith in God, Jesus, or the trustworthiness of the Bible, to realize that in all likelihood the holy writer (whether Moses, "J", "J1", "J2", or whoever) found the basic elements of an ancient Sumerian document to be the ideal vehicle for expressing the theological truths that the Holy Spirit desired that writer to write.

Though the fall cannot be proved, we can observe certain "arguments" that humanity is not what it should be. A glance in the mirror or at the headlines of the daily paper tells us we are not functioning ideally, either in isolation or in community. We can envision something better, both for us and for the world. Jesus has delivered, and will call us into, that "something better". Such "arguments" are from faith to faith. Another person, looking at the same "evidence", might say, "No, all is as it should be. This is all there is, and this is the way it is. Your 'something better' is an illusion." That might be called an argument from non-faith to non-faith.

The "happy frustration" of the faithful with their human limitations in getting at iron-clad answers for questions like these is summarized by the writer of Ecclesiastes
when he says:

> [God] has made everything beautiful in
> its time; also he has put eternity into
> man's mind, yet so that he cannot find
> out what God has done from the beginning
> to the end.
>
> Ecclesiastes 3:11

PRIORITIES IN THE CHRISTIAN MESSAGE

If any of this answer is correct, then why didn't anyone ever tell me these things before? Why didn't anyone
ever suggest that there is more than one creation account?
Why didn't anyone ever hint at this information about Sumerian records? Why don't pastors talk about these things
in sermons?

I'll tell you why. It's a matter of priorities. The
information we've discussed in this book has been known and
written about for a long time now. One pastor or theologian
may discount the possibility that any of it is true; another
may embrace it. Both are aware that this body of information
exists, but neither would find it a suitable topic for presentation at a worship service. The priority subject of the
Church's public proclamation is Jesus Christ and him crucified; Jesus and human relationships; Jesus and human destiny;
Jesus and the grace of God. As the service is usually struc-
tured, and as its purpose is usually conceived, there is
simply not time or opportunity to get deeply into matters of
lesser priority.

I am not saying that the question about creation and
evolution is not a good one. It is a good one, and an important one, but only to the extent that a person is asking
the question. It can be answered adequately only as there

113

is time and opportunity for a complete answer. This is a
rather short book, but see how long it has taken to communi-
cate with reasonable completeness the answer that works for
me. None of the answer is especially good or helpful without all of it. Think how disturbing and unfair it would be
all around if a Christian worshiper heard in a sermon just
a stray line from here or there in this book. His impres-
sion could easily be, "The preacher says Genesis 1 and 2
contradict each other", or, "The preacher says Adam and Eve
are just pagan fables", or "The preacher says Christians
can't be certain about anything." I haven't said any of
those things, but that is the sort of disturbance that could
be set off if there were not time to give a more complete
answer to a good question.

Certainly the topic of creation and evolution would be
appropriate for a Christian classroom situation, but for a
sermon? Probably not. There just wouldn't be enough time
in the twenty minutes or so usually allotted to the sermon
to get to the full and winning presentation of what the
faith is all about, Jesus Christ and him crucified. Even
in the Christian classroom, however, unless the question is
really being asked, unless it's a priority item, this may
be the kind of information that many Christians could very
well live without.

This study of the creation accounts is important to me,
however, because friends of mine have asked me for the full-
est and straightest answer I can give. To you the study may
be merely another person's thoughts on an interesting subject, or it may be a real help in getting past a point of
"blockage" to a fuller.Christian faith. For someone else,
it may be an exercise in Biblical interpretation. For still
another person, it may be a question of no importance at all.

"On the one hand, gentlemen, never hold anything back
from your people, as though they were too limited to handle
certain privileged information. On the other hand, don't
go about upsetting people just to prove how knowledgeable
you are." That was only a chance remark by one of my men-
tors in a seminary classroom, way back when, but I've always
thought it was very profound advice.

114

Let us end as we began. To search and probe the creation accounts as we have done is not to undermine God, Church, or Bible. It is rather to come to renewed faith in God who creates and sustains heaven and earth. Whatever else has proved helpful and useful to you in this book, may that strengthened and renewed faith be yours!

Let us doubt without disbelief the things to be believed.

NOTES

[1]Lueker, Erwin L., Ed. in Chief. Lutheran Cyclopedia. St. Louis, Concordia Publishing House, 1954. "Inspiration, Doctrine Of", pages 511-514. The first sentence of the article reads, in its entirety:

> By confessing the doctrine of inspiration, we declare our belief - based on the words of the Bible itself - that the Holy Spirit exercised a special influence by which He guided His chosen instruments to speak the things He desired them to speak, and to write the things He desired them to write, in the precise manner and in the very words in which He desired these things to be spoken or written.

[2]Hinz, Richard T. (Harold W. Rast, Ed.) Journey to Freedom: Teacher's Guide. Concordia Publishing House: St. Louis, 1971. See especially page 43.

[3]I have been given to understand, in no uncertain terms, by a woman friend, that Eve's being created at the end of the second account does not make her an "afterthought" of God. It was simply that God was "saving the best for last". Her understanding is corroborated by a (male) theologian

friend who advises me that womankind is consistently elevated in all those parts of the Pentateuch ascribed to this "Yahwist" writer. Male chauvinists, you are forewarned!

[4]Guirand, Felix (Ed.). _The New Larousse Encyclopedia of Mythology._ (Richard Aldington and Delano Ames, translators). The Hamlyn Publishing Group, Ltd.: London, 1968. See especially their chapters on "Assyro-Babylonian Mythology", pages 48 and following; and on the Egyptian gods, pages 11-28.

[5]The ancient near eastern tradition that man was created from the blood clot of a deceased divinity is preserved and perpetuated not in Christianity but in Islam. In the Qu'ran, Surrah (chapter) 96 praises God who created man "from a clot of blood".

[6]Kramer, Samuel Noah. _History Begins at Sumer._ Doubleday and Company, Inc. (Doubleday Anchor Books): Garden City, New York, 1959. See especially Chapter 13, "Man's First Cosmogony and Cosmology", pages 76-103. See also, "Paradise: The First Biblical Parallels", pages 143-149.

[7]Connell, The Rev. Francis J. _The New Confraternity Edition Revised: Baltimore Catechism and Mass._ Benziger Brothers, Inc.: New York, 1949 (Imprimatur for the new edition, 1958).

[8]De Chardin, Pierre Teilhard. _The Phenomenon of Man._ Harper and Row (Harper Torchbooks): New York, 1965.

[9]Von Däniken, Erich. _Chariots of the Gods?_ and _Gods from Outer Space._ Bantam Books, Inc.: New York, 1972.

[10]Habel, Norman C. _The Form and Meaning of the Fall Narrative: A Detailed Analysis of Genesis 3._ Concordia Seminary Print Shop: 801 De Mun Ave., St. Louis, Mo., 1965.

11Buttrick, George Arthur (editor). The Interpreter's
Bible, Volume I. Abingdon Press: New York and Nashville,
1952. See especially the article, "The Growth of the Hexa-
teuch", by Cuthbert A. Simpson, pages 185-200; "The Faith
of Israel", by G. Ernest Wright, pages 349-389 (particularly
pages 367-370; 384-387); "Genesis: Introduction", by Cuthbert A. Simpson, pages 439-457 (particularly pages 441-447:
453); and the exegesis of Genesis 3, also by Cuthbert A.
Simpson, pages 501-516.

S83

$3.85 Alex Pub Hs.